MARKETING SHORTCUTS

for the

SELF-EMPLOYED

MARKETING SHORTCUTS

for the
SELF-EMPLOYED

Leverage Resources, Establish Online Credibility, and Crush Your Competition

Patrick Schwerdtfeger

WILEY

John Wiley and Sons, Inc.

Published by John Wiley and Sons, Inc., Hoboken, New Jersey.
Published simultaneously in Canada.

For general information on our other products and services or for technical support, please contact our Customer Care Department within the United States at (800) 762-2974, outside the United States at (317) 572-3993 or fax (317) 572-4002.

Wiley also publishes its books in a variety of electronic formats. Some content that appears in print may not be available in electronic books. For more information about Wiley products, visit our website at www.wiley.com.

ISBN 978-1-118-01420-2 (cloth)
ISBN 978-1-118-07805-1 (ebk)
ISBN 978-1-118-07806-8 (ebk)
ISBN 978-1-118-07807-5 (ebk)

Printed in the United States of America

10 9 8 7 6 5 4 3 2 1

To my dad

Contents

Acknowledgments

There are, of course, many people to thank but I need to start with those who played the most significant role. To my agent, Michael Larsen, your guidance made this possible. To my editor, Lauren Murphy, you walked me through the process. Thank you both for your kindness, patience, and professionalism.

Many others played a part in the compilation of this book by editing, providing ideas, or offering direction. They include David Mitroff, Rob and Emily Ludlow, Scott Cooney, and Tom Loarie.

My career as a speaker and the success that stems from people recommending me and my programs is why I now have a book deal. Among many others, my recommenders include Amy Sluss, Ann Evanston, Bryan Clark, Cathleen Hoffman, Christopher Henley, Chrystal Bougon, Deb Droz, Edith Yeung, Ellen Looyen, Gina Harper, Hope Desroches, Jeffrey Slayter, Jessica Thurmond-Pohlonski, Karen Clark, Kathleen Mozena, Lennart Svanberg, Lise Bodine, Luanne Stevenson, Michael Loschke, Rajeev Kohli, and Sahar Kordahi. I am grateful for your trust.

Part One

Define Your Business Model

Chapter 1

Introduction

Let's jump right in.

More than 100 million people are using Twitter today. Are most of them wasting their time? Absolutely! A lot of people are singing the praises of online marketing and social media these days, but much of it is just a bunch of hype. These people might be having fun. They might be "being social." But they're not finding new clients for their business. They're certainly not growing their revenue. A *few* people and businesses, however, are taking advantage of the opportunities presented by these new communication tools; they are using simple but powerful strategies to explode their revenue virtually overnight.

That *is* happening. Those stories *are* true. So what exactly are they doing? What strategies are they using? What tactics are delivering measurable results? Answering these questions is what this book is about. It's about isolating the success stories. It's about identifying the strategies and tactics that work.

The book also evolved out of my own countless experiments, many of them failures, over seven years of self-employed life. My goal was to build credibility and exposure, and I tried everything! Some of my efforts succeeded. Most didn't. The chapters ahead cover the strategies that actually worked. Will they work in every situation and for every business? No. But they've all been successful for one business or another, and that means they're worth testing on your own business too.

This book tells you how to get things done. You'll notice the contents are divided into 80 chapters, each with a narrow and specific focus. You can read each chapter in less than 10 minutes and quickly gain an understanding of the strategy as well as its implementation process. Each chapter (except this one) concludes with an itemized to-do list, allowing you to break the topic into specific tasks and see results quickly.

The chapters are presented in a specific order. You can waste an enormous amount of time doing things in the wrong order. More than half the value in this book is the sequential presentation. Regardless of where your business is today, you will benefit by starting at the beginning and working your way through the book. Together, we will align your business with today's realities and tomorrow's opportunities. More than ever before, those opportunities are available and accessible to anyone who's willing to do the work.

Here's the sad reality: most people don't do anything. They never take action. They say they will but they don't. They get excited but it fades. As a result, most people never see real results and eventually get discouraged and give up. You can get the best advice in the world but it won't do you any good unless you take action. This book offers dozens of simple but powerful strategies, but the actual implementation is up to you.

Please commit to this process. Create a folder and track your progress. Go through the steps and embrace curiosity when confronting the unfamiliar. The strategies presented in this book are here because they produce results. Together, we'll build a strategic foundation for your business that's far more sophisticated than most businesses ever achieve. Together, we'll take steps that will leave your business far better positioned than it is today.

The first section of this book is devoted to defining your business model. This may seem unrelated to modern marketing but nothing could be further from the truth. A clear and focused business model is essential to effective Internet positioning. Everybody uses the Internet differently. We all have our own favorite platforms and our own way of accessing information. But the one thing that remains constant for all of us is the mechanism of finding information online. Search engines and social media platforms are rewarding websites that offer extensive but focused information about their topic. The websites that shine are those that present a clear purpose with easily understood benefits and a landslide of good information. These websites can only be built by companies that have a well-defined business focus.

Work through the first few chapters and do the suggested exercises. They will force you to hone your business model and fine-tune your value proposition. That clarity adds to your business foundation and pays dividends online and off. Success breeds success! Share this book with your business colleagues and work through the steps together. You might be surprised how different their experiences and ideas are from your own. Not only will you benefit from their unique perspective but you'll have more fun along the way. The Twitter hashtag (explained in Chapter 59) for this book is #80shortcuts. Please include it in all related tweets.

Now, let's get down to business!

Chapter 2

Develop Expertise

Are you an expert?

The answer is *yes*! Yes, you are. You're an expert. On what? I don't know. That's what we need to figure out. The truth is, everyone is an expert at something . . . even *you*. And whether you realize it or not, thousands of people are searching for your expertise to improve their lives or build their businesses. My first book, *Make Yourself Useful: Marketing in the 21st Century* was all about being an expert and providing value. In today's information society, you need to carve out a little slice of the universe and claim it as your own. You need to decide what your specialty is and become an expert in that field.

A common phrase in Internet marketing circles is "go an inch wide and a mile deep," referring to the importance of a clearly focused specialization. Search engines such as Google love narrow little niches that people dominate with massive expertise. Pick a specific topic and become an expert in that field! In a 2004 article published in *Wired* magazine, Chris Anderson coined the term "long tail" to describe this same idea. He was referring to the advantages of exploiting super specific niches on the Internet. He later elaborated on the idea in his book *The Long Tail: Why the Future of Business is Selling Less of More* (2006, Hyperion).

This process of establishing your qualifications as an expert involves the following steps:

1. Pick a narrow specific topic.
2. Acquire massive expertise.
3. Present yourself as an expert.

6

I'll leave step 1 to you, and we'll deal with step 3 in the next chapter. But step 2 is tactical. Step 2 is structural. We can begin tackling step 2 right now. We'll start with an exercise that will take some time, but will yield amazing results. First pick a few keywords to describe your specialty, then do the following:

- Go to EzineArticles.com and do a search for the keywords you chose to describe your area of expertise. You'll find thousands of free articles other people have written about your topic. Browse the titles and read the articles that catch your attention.
- Go to the iTunes Music Store, click on Podcasts, then do a Power Search using your keywords. You'll find hundreds of free podcasts about your topic. Sort the results by popularity and subscribe to the top ones. Listen to the podcasts while commuting to work or getting some exercise at the gym.
- Go to YouTube and do a search for "how to" and the same keywords. You'll find incredible free videos people have made about your topic. Watch the videos and learn. Not only will you be introduced to your competition but you'll gain tremendous expertise in the process.

This exercise demonstrates the nearly limitless resources available at your fingertips. It also helps you refine your specialty. You'll see what others are already doing and, more important, you'll see what they're *not* doing—at least not yet. Pick your topic. Stake your claim. Start building your expertise.

Implementation Checklist

☐ Decide on a field you can specialize in.
☐ Select a few keywords for your specialty.
☐ Use your keywords to find articles on EzineArticles.
☐ Use your keywords to find podcasts on iTunes.
☐ Use your keywords to find videos on YouTube.
☐ Make notes and build your expertise.
☐ Notice what your competition is doing.
☐ Notice what your competition is *not* doing.
☐ Compare notes and ideas with a colleague.

Chapter 3

Belief Systems

Are you sabotaging your own success?

When it comes to growing your business, one of the most important things you can do is get your belief systems in check. If you don't, your own limiting beliefs can turn you into your own worst enemy.

This happens a lot, and most of the time, you're not even aware of the undermining effects those limiting beliefs are having. Whether you realize it or not, your belief systems define almost everything you do.

Consider Figure 3.1. Your *Beliefs* form the foundation of your *Decisions*. Your *Decisions* lead to your *Actions*. Your *Actions* define your *Results*. And your *Results* feed back into your *Beliefs*.

On May 6, 1954, Roger Bannister ran a mile in less than 4 minutes for the first time in human history. It had never been done before. Many doctors had even believed the human heart was incapable of enduring such an incredible strain. They were wrong.

But . . . Bannister's time was bested just 46 days later. And during the next three years, 16 athletes ran a mile in less than 4 minutes, and hundreds more have broken the 4-minute mile since then. As of this writing, the current record is 3 minutes and 43 seconds.

What changed? The belief system.

Up until the day Bannister ran the 4-minute mile, nobody believed it was possible. Once someone proved that it *was* possible, the belief system changed. After that, the mental barrier was gone and the new results reflected the new beliefs.

Improving your belief systems is a never-ending process. Even if you're already successful, I'm willing to bet there's still a gap between where you

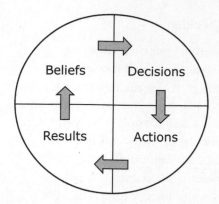

FIGURE 3.1   The Cognitive Execution Cycle

are and where you'd like to be. Different people and different programs advocate different approaches.

Law of Attraction programs start in the *Beliefs* quadrant. By imagining and focusing on what you want, you can trick your mind into a different belief system and that can roll through the circle and improve your results.

A lot of motivational speakers start in the *Decisions* quadrant. By making a single decision—a decision to take action—you can change your life forever. The self-help author and speaker Anthony Robbins espouses this philosophy, and the statement is true. One decision can indeed change everything.

Some even start in the *Results* quadrant. By pretending as if you're already there—and living like it—you can get some traction and start a domino effect that improves the level of your performance (but that's a risky approach).

This book starts in the *Actions* quadrant. It focuses on the specific tactics that get results. If you know which actions deliver results, changing your beliefs is easy.

Regardless of the approach, you need to start a deliberate program to ensure you actually *believe* you're an expert. If you don't, you'll end up sabotaging your own efforts and making it harder to achieve the goals you've set for yourself.

Believing in yourself is easier said than done. Confidence grows out of an established pattern of success. The purpose of this book is to help you establish that pattern. You'll find that small steps and small victories add up quickly.

Implementation Checklist

- ☐ Take ownership of your own expertise.
- ☐ Select which quadrant you'll focus on first.
    - ☐ If it's *Beliefs*, start visualizing your success.
    - ☐ If it's *Decisions*, make that decision today.
    - ☐ If it's *Actions*, start mapping out your plan.
    - ☐ If it's *Results*, be careful—this is risky.
- ☐ Focus only on your desired destination.
- ☐ Establish a pattern of success.
- ☐ Compare notes and ideas with a colleague.

Chapter 4

Problems + PAIN = Profit

Are your customers ready to spend money?

To answer that question, you might want to think about a brilliant little equation coined by Christine Comaford, author of *Rules for Renegades: How to Make More Money, Rock Your Career, and Revel in Your Individuality* (McGraw-Hill, 2007). It's so true . . .

$$Problems + PAIN = Profit$$

There are two basic requirements for a successful business model. Many businesses meet only one requirement. Many more have neither! If you want to build your business, you need to make absolutely sure that you have both. First, you need a problem that you can solve. That's obvious. There needs to be something wrong, a lack or a need that's not being met. Take a look at your area of expertise and ask yourself where the problems are. What's missing? What doesn't work properly? What are people always struggling with? Write down your answers.

Second, people need to be in *pain* because of the problem. This is important. There are lots of problems that nobody cares about. Many problems don't result in pain. And because of that, people aren't willing to spend their hard-earned money to fix them. You need to find the people who are in *pain*. Who is suffering? That's your target market. That's your audience. That's your ideal customer. That's who is looking for you and is ready to spend money on your product or service.

This calculation may sound trivial, but most companies never go through this basic exercise and it affects their sales potential directly. If you get a clear picture of exactly what problem you solve and what *pain* you alleviate, all of your marketing efforts will immediately become more effective. Set some time aside—maybe 30 minutes or an hour—to ask yourself these questions. Put your work into your file. We'll be coming back to it in the chapters ahead and taking the next steps.

Implementation Checklist

- [ ] Identify the problem your product solves.
- [ ] Describe the *pain* caused by the problem.
- [ ] Note the emotional distress you alleviate.
- [ ] Focus marketing on emotional benefits.
- [ ] Compare notes and ideas with a colleague.

Chapter 5

Value Proposition

So . . . what do you sell?

In the last chapter, we isolated the problem your product or service addresses. More importantly, we identified the *pain* caused by the problem. The people who experience that pain are your target market. They're the ones who are ready to spend money on your product or service. The next step is to identify and understand exactly what your product or service is. What do you sell? Specifically. Is it a silly question? Let's take a closer look.

Does Starbucks sell coffee? I would say *no,* not really. Starbucks sells an environment, an experience. When McDonald's introduced a variety of high-end coffees, were they really competing with Starbucks? No, they weren't. In fact, they didn't even pretend to compete.

McDonald's realized that some people go to Starbucks to buy fancy coffee but don't care about the Starbucks experience at all. If they could provide a similar product for less money, they could steal those customers. And they were right. But they never tried to compete with Starbucks' value proposition. McDonald's sells a few high-end coffees. Starbucks sells an experience. Two different things. The options appeal to two entirely different audiences. To that end, McDonald's specifically addressed the unpretentiousness of their specialty coffees in their advertising campaign.

If you really want to grow your business, you need to focus your marketing efforts on the customer experience, not your product's features. You don't sell your product's features. You sell your product's *benefits.* An even better way of looking at it: you sell the *emotions* your customers experience when they use your product. Think back to our discussion about pain in Chapter 4. What you're selling is the alleviation of that pain. You're selling the emotions your customers experience when the pain is

13

finally gone. In the case of Starbucks, they're selling a feeling of comfort, a tiny little vacation people go on every time they step into a Starbucks store. Their customers escape their lives, even if just for a moment. They take time to breathe. They leave the craziness behind and take a short vacation with their tasty Starbucks coffee.

Think about the emotions your product delivers. You'll need to define those emotional benefits before the next chapter, where we'll be working on your 30-second elevator pitch. So get a pen and paper. Jot down some notes. And figure out exactly what you sell.

Implementation Checklist

- ☐ List all your product (or service) features.
- ☐ Identify a benefit for each feature.
- ☐ Describe an emotion for each benefit.
- ☐ Define your business in terms of emotions.
- ☐ Focus all marketing on those emotions.
- ☐ Compare notes and ideas with a colleague.

Chapter 6

Elevator Pitch

What's your elevator pitch?

Let's start with a definition. An "elevator pitch" is a really concise way of describing what your company does. Usually 90 words or less, the elevator pitch was given its name because you should be able to tell someone exactly what you do in the time it takes to ride an elevator together—about 30 seconds. Yet again, the vast majority of companies don't have this simple but essential positioning statement in place. They never took the time to put it into words. They never took the time to define their business model in clear concise language.

We're not going to make that mistake.

Your elevator pitch is a metaphorical equivalent of your business focus. Most businesses don't have a true focus. Taking the time to write an effective elevator pitch forces you to find your focus. Your elevator pitch forms the foundation for your entire business and, in particular, all of your online marketing efforts. Before we start crafting your pitch and identifying your focus, we need to define the objective. What are we actually trying to accomplish with the elevator pitch? This is important! From what you tell people in the pitch, you want them to *know* what you sell, *want* what you sell, and *buy* what you sell—and you have just 30 seconds to get all that across. Needless to say, you need to use every second wisely. You need a strategy. You need every word to play a role. So here's what to do: Write your elevator pitch one sentence at a time. There are four sentences in all.

Sentence 1 needs to identify who you are. Start by taking the following format: "Hello, my name is XXX and I am a(n) YYY specializing in ZZZ." I know it's simple but it's a start. You can refine it later.

Sentence 2 needs to describe your specialty in more detail. But it needs to do more than that. It also needs to identify the problem that exists and how you solve that problem. Here's where we bring in the *pain* we identified in Chapter 4. Identify the problem and explain how your product alleviates the *pain* caused by the problem.

Sentence 3 needs to differentiate you from your competition. Why are you better? What makes you different? You need to use this sentence to establish credibility, build value, and provide proof. If you have statistics to back up your claim, include them. If other products are more expensive, say so. If you deliver better results, make that clear.

And finally, *Sentence 4* needs to give a call to action. Tell people what to do next. Be specific. What action do you want them to take? Say it! This is often the most difficult part but it's also the most important. Tell them exactly what to do to get the process started. People like direction and hate surprises. Be confident and be honest. Tell them what to do next.

Now, put all of your sentences together. Write it all in paragraph format and read it to yourself. Make adjustments and try different words. When you're happy with it, read it to your friends and work colleagues. Read it to people who have no idea what you do and ask them if your four-sentence elevator pitch makes it clear. Here are a couple last-minute tips.

First, don't say too much. Make sure your pitch is 90 words or less; 75 words would be ideal. It needs to be precise and quick—no run-on sentences. Clear simple statements. That's it. Second, dumb it down. Seriously. Get rid of the jargon words, even the ones you think everybody should know. Not everyone knows them. People who are not in your field don't know those "easy" words. So take them out. Your pitch needs to be written at a sixth-grade level. Simple, simple. You want an 11-year-old child to hear your pitch and understand what you do.

This project is far more important than you might think. Your elevator pitch forms the basis for everything else you do. In the next chapter, we'll start defining your target market. Once you know exactly what you do and where your target market is, you're in business!

Implementation Checklist

- ☐ Allocate time to write your elevator pitch.
- ☐ Sentence 1: Identify yourself.
- ☐ Sentence 2: What *pain* you alleviate.
- ☐ Sentence 3: Why are you better?
- ☐ Sentence 4: Give a call to action!
- ☐ Make adjustments and refine your pitch over time.
- ☐ Compare notes and ideas with a colleague.

Chapter 7

Target Market

Where are your customers?

No business can succeed without customers! If you're in the process of starting or growing your business, it can't hurt to set some time aside and really try to understand your audience and where they are. Before we begin, let's review the past few chapters. In Chapter 4, we identified the problem your product solves. But more importantly, we looked at the *pain* people feel as a result of that problem. It's the people who feel that pain who are ready to spend money.

In Chapter 5, we looked at the business model in slightly more philosophical terms. What exactly do you sell? Answering this question is important because a lot of businesses think they sell features. They don't. They sell benefits, sort of. They actually sell the *emotional feeling* people experience when they use the product. When marketing your product, don't communicate the features, at least not right at the beginning. Don't even focus on the benefits. That's not the most important thing. Tell people about the emotional feeling! That's what will motivate them to buy. In Chapter 6, we pulled it together and crafted a 30-second elevator pitch. This four-sentence pitch identifies who you are, what the problem is, how you solve the problem, what makes you different, and what people should do to take action.

Now, let's look at a few tools you can use to find your target market. Whether you want to market your product online or offline, the Internet provides some great resources to help you understand your customers. Start by visiting the free Google keyword selector tool. To find it, search for "google keyword tool" on Google. It should be the first listing. Once at the Google tool, you can enter a few keywords that relate to your product and quickly get a long list of related words and phrases. Sort the results by

Global Search Volume and you can immediately see what people are searching for most often in your area of expertise. This simple technique is incredibly useful. Within seconds you can see exactly what people are searching for and it will also give you some insight as to where you might find those people.

This type of market research was never possible before. The Internet has opened up a new world of transparency. In the offline world, you had to do focus groups or surveys to understand what your market was thinking. No longer. Today, you can visit this free tool any time you like and get direct access to the exact preferences of the population. You can also visit http://directory.big-boards.com and search for the same keywords. This site lists forums and discussion boards where people are talking about your topic. Conversations are markets on today's social Internet. (We'll talk more about that in Chapter 44.) If you want to access a market, participate in the conversation.

One of the biggest forums on the Internet is Yahoo! Answers. Once logged in, you can either ask questions or provide answers to other people's questions. This is a spectacular place to touch your audience. If you answer questions you know answers to, your contribution will be viewed by precisely those people looking for that information. (We'll go into more detail about posting at Yahoo! and Amazon in Chapter 54.) This is one of the best things about the Internet. On almost any interactive website, you can isolate your target market with unparalleled precision by simply demonstrating your own expertise in the public domain. The only people who will find your contribution are those people who are looking specifically for that information.

I also recommend putting your keywords into a Google search and seeing what comes up. Whatever shows up is what your customers are finding. Review the search results. Those are your biggest online competitors. Look at the right-hand column of "sponsored links." That's what other people are trying to sell your audience. Think about what your customers have in common. What are their interests? What's their profession? What other activities do they participate in? The more you know about your audience, the more ideas you'll have for finding them.

Sometimes your first instinct isn't the best choice. If you're trying to promote yourself as an Internet marketing consultant, for example, a forum about Internet marketing wouldn't necessarily serve you well. A forum like that would be full of your competitors. Instead, a forum for small business owners or financial advisors or real estate agents or chiropractors or dentists would be a much better place to look for prospective customers. Those are the people who probably need an Internet marketing consultant.

The people on the Internet marketing forums are already tapping into online marketing channels. Look for groups on Facebook or LinkedIn. Look for clubs on Meetup or Yahoo! Groups. Search for the top bloggers on Technorati. All of these activities help you isolate your target market. If you're unfamiliar with any of these websites, fear not. There are chapters on each one later in the book. If you're dying of curiosity, feel free to jump ahead to learn more; put a sticky note on this page and come back to it later.

Start compiling a list of all the online places where you'll find people interested in your field. As you work through future chapters, this list will determine where you spend your time.

Implementation Checklist

- ☐ Visit the free Google keyword tool.
- ☐ Learn what your market is searching for.
- ☐ Visit the Big-Boards forum directory.
- ☐ Find the biggest online forums in your field.
- ☐ Put your keywords into a Google search.
- ☐ See who your biggest competitors are.
- ☐ Read the "sponsored links" on Google.
- ☐ Search for groups on Facebook and LinkedIn.
- ☐ Search clubs on Meetup and Yahoo! Groups.
- ☐ Search top bloggers on Technorati.com.
- ☐ Make note of the good potential markets.
- ☐ Compare notes and ideas with a colleague.

Chapter 8

List of Prospects

Now that your business is almost ready to launch, who will you call first?

You would be amazed how many businesses try to launch before they have assembled a list of potential prospects. Don't waste precious time and money attempting to get sales without building a list first. If your customers are all in a single profession, your job is fairly easy. For example, let's say you plan to sell your product to dentists or auto mechanics or lawyers. You can quickly go to switchboard.com or yellowpages.com and do a search for those keywords. These websites then offer you a list of categories to refine your search. By selecting a particular category and entering a zip code, you can immediately get a list of all your prospects in that area. Of course, the list will probably span multiple pages with only 10 listings on each page. But with a little patience, along with the copy and paste functions on your computer, you can transfer all that information into an Excel spreadsheet in an hour or two. In Excel, you can manipulate the data and organize it into different columns or categories. Is it a menial job? Sure. But the list is invaluable; the time spent is well worth it.

I did this back in 2002. I was compiling a list of escrow officers for my notary business and used switchboard.com to do so. In less than two hours, I had a list of 200 local escrow offices in an Excel spreadsheet with columns for company name, street address, city name, state, zip code, phone number, and fax number. Done. That list then determined who I introduced myself to. It became the foundation of my business. As I visited those offices, I collected business cards and added specific contact names for each. I then imported the list into my content management software and used that database to manage my business. But it all started with that tedious two-hour copy and paste job!

Here's another golden secret that will help you as you compile your list of prospects. You may be familiar with a company called InfoUSA. They maintain an enormous database and sell lists to paying customers. As it turns out, you can go to your public library and access a database called ReferenceUSA, a sister company to InfoUSA that is paid for by the government. What does that mean? It means you can get the exact same data for free that InfoUSA sells. The only downside is that you're usually restricted in terms of the number of listings you can download in one sitting. Other than that, it's exactly the same. ReferenceUSA is an incredibly powerful resource and it doesn't cost a penny. It's one of the best kept secrets I'm aware of. Take advantage of it. Schedule an hour to visit your local library and ask the person at the Reference Desk to show you how to access and use this resource.

In many cases, you can access ReferenceUSA from your home computer with a library card number and your last name. Once logged in, you can sort on a variety of different criteria and quickly put a list together that will let you and your business hit the ground running. It's worth noting that recent budget cuts have reduced the number of libraries providing ReferenceUSA. In the San Francisco Bay Area (where I live), only a handful of libraries still have it. Ask at your local library; if they don't have it, they'll let you know where to go.

Lastly, do a few Google searches for your keywords and the word "directory." Most industries have public online directories. When I first opened Box14 Financial, a company that liquidated seller financing notes, I compiled a list of more than 5,500 business brokers across the country. It only took about four hours—all because I found two online directories and was able to copy and paste the entire list to my own computer. Once you have your list compiled in Excel, import it into your contact management system (like ACT! or Goldmine or Salesforce.com). Growing your business is a lot easier when you have a list of prospects. Compiling the list is a tedious job but you only have to do it once. Set some time aside to do the research. When it's all done, you'll be happy you did.

Implementation Checklist

- ☐ Search your keywords on switchboard.com.
- ☐ Search your keywords on yellowpages.com.
- ☐ Ask for ReferenceUSA at your local library.
- ☐ Google your keywords plus "directory."
- ☐ Copy and paste the information into Excel.
- ☐ Organize the data into a series of columns.
- ☐ Import your list into a contact management system.
- ☐ Compare notes and ideas with a colleague.

Chapter 9

E-mail Distribution Lists

What's the most valuable thing in your business?

In many cases, it's your e-mail list. Why is this list so powerful? Because you can click "send" and have your message reach potentially thousands (or even hundreds of thousands) of people in an instant, and it won't cost you a penny. If you ever try to sell your business, you'll get far more if you have a big e-mail list. It's a sales channel. It's a communication channel. It's a direct link with qualified prospects. If you could do only one thing to build a stable and profitable business, build an e-mail list!

We'll talk more about building your own e-mail list in Chapters 23 and 50. For now, I'd like to introduce the available options. There are basically three different ways to market your product or service by e-mail:

1. E-mail to your own list.
2. E-mail to a joint venture list.
3. E-mail to a distribution list.

Your Own List

E-mailing to your own list is just that. You send out a message to a list of e-mail addresses you've accumulated on your own. There are some great strategies for using your own list; we'll go over them in later chapters, after we've covered a few website topics.

Joint Ventures

Here's how this type of e-mail marketing works: You approach someone in your field who already has a big e-mail list and then send a message out to

24

that person's or company's list, splitting the resulting revenue. It's a great way to get your products in front of a huge audience quickly.

But it's not always that easy.

The people who have developed large e-mail lists are in a powerful position. Everyone solicits their help and they can cherry-pick the people and products they support. As a result, they can be very demanding. It's very common for good joint venture (JV) partners to require a substantial split of the revenue. If you're selling information products (such as how-to PDF documents, educational videos, etc.), the JV partner's cut can be as high as 50 or 75 percent. Why? Because information products delivered digitally over the Internet have no cost. Once they're created, they can be delivered to an unlimited number of people for no additional unit cost. JV partners are well aware of that and, as a result, demand a higher percentage of the revenue.

By the way, don't expect to see their list. Those with big lists are fiercely protective over them and will commit to sending out the promotional e-mail on your behalf, but nothing more. You just give them the text you want to send and they'll do the rest.

Let's break down the strategy. You're not getting their list. You're just renting it. But if someone buys your product, you obviously get all of the buyer's contact information at the point of sale. So the idea is to do JV deals when you're making an irresistible offer that will generate a big response. That way, you're building your own list with all the people who accept the offer. There's always a bit of a balancing act because the list owner wants to make money on the deal. That means he or she probably won't be very happy if you basically just offer something for super cheap or even free. In fact, he or she probably won't allow it at all. Usually, people offer a "front-end" product—something cheap with impressive value—and a "back-end" product that costs more money. The initial e-mail promotes the front-end product and those who purchase it are offered an up-sell for the (usually more expensive) back-end product. The list owner usually makes a higher percentage on the front-end product and then a smaller percentage on the back-end product. That way, you both achieve what you wanted. You get a big response and the list owner makes money on the campaign.

Find out who the big list owners are in your field. Subscribe to their lists so you get an idea of the products they're promoting. And when you have your own product ready to go, try soliciting them with a JV proposal. If they see real value and an opportunity to make money, they might accept your proposal and send your offer out to tens of thousands of people.

Distribution Lists

In many industries, there are e-mail distribution lists already established where you can send out your e-mail message for a flat fee. The nice thing about JV campaigns is that you pay only a percentage of revenue. If you sell nothing, it costs you nothing. With distribution lists, however, you pay a flat fee regardless of the response you get. But unlike JV campaigns, if you do make sales, you keep all the profit! The other thing to keep in mind is that JV lists are based on an actual human relationship; as a result, JV lists tend to convert into sales much better than distribution lists, which are designed exclusively for marketing purposes and sold to anyone willing to pay the fee. Nevertheless, distribution lists offer real opportunities in the right situation and are worth testing in your business too.

A good friend of mine sends out e-mails to a list of 60,000 independent distributors in the promotional products industry for a flat fee of just $275. He's been very successful for the past eight years and has built his entire business on this one marketing strategy. I recently found a list of 72,000 mortgage brokers that can be e-mailed for $1,800. That's a lot more than $275, but (depending on your sales) it's still a lot less than a joint venture campaign would cost you.

You could also use a company such as Majon.com. They have lists of more than 20 million names and you can send an e-mail to the entire list for about $2,000. Obviously, you pay less when the list is completely unfiltered, but it's still tempting to send an e-mail to 20 million people! You might be asking yourself, are distribution lists spam? Well, if they're "opt-in" lists, technically they're not. What's opt-in? It's a list where subscribers voluntarily opted in to receive e-mails. But even still, it's pretty close to spam. Yes, there's potential, but you don't want to come across as a spammer either. My advice? Test it once or twice and see what reaction you get.

Do some research. Put your keywords into a Google search along with the words "e-mail distribution list" and see what comes up. You might be surprised at the result. In the case of my friend, he built his entire business with a single e-mail campaign.

Think about the potential for a distribution list e-mail campaign. What could you offer?

Resist the temptation to be greedy. Most people who are new to the Internet are too quick to ask for money. The trend is toward providing more value upfront and building trust first. Save the sales pitch for later. Think about an irresistible offer; something anyone would want. The goal is interaction. You want to engage your community. You want your audience to recognize who you are and become familiar with your name. Remember this important equation:

$$Interaction = Trust$$

The more your potential customers interact with you, the more they'll trust you. We'll talk about this in later chapters, but for now keep in mind that you need to treat your e-mail campaign like a sales funnel. Offer tons of value at the beginning and build trust with your audience. Without trust, you'll never get any sales anyway. E-mail distribution lists are powerful opportunities to get your message out quickly and affordably. Do the research and see what you can find. Take a chance. It could change your business forever.

Implementation Checklist

- ☐ Find the online gurus in your field.
- ☐ Subscribe to their e-mail lists.
- ☐ Make note of the products they're selling.
- ☐ Google "e-mail distribution lists."
- ☐ Identify irresistible offers for your audience.
- ☐ Build trust first; make money afterward.
- ☐ Send out a huge e-mail blast . . . and wait.
- ☐ Compare notes and ideas with a colleague.

Chapter 10

Write a Business Plan

Do you have a business plan?

Don't worry, I'm not going to guilt you into writing a business plan. This chapter is different than what you're probably expecting. No, I'm not going to push you into extensive market research. No, I'm not going to tell you that a business plan is essential to success. It isn't, but it has a place. Let me explain. Most of what I try fails. At least 80 percent of my efforts crash and burn. So why write a big business plan? Once my experiment fails, I'll just have to write a new one anyway, right? Writing a big plan is futile and takes too long. I don't have time. It just isn't worth it for me, at least not during the experimental phase.

What do I mean by experimental phase? I'm talking about the time *before* you've identified a sustainable business model. When people fantasize about starting a business, they always start their planning at the point where they already have a sustainable business model, and then they plan all the exciting ways they plan to grow that business model and turn it into a thriving empire. Problem is, most businesses never reach that point. The vast majority of new businesses fail way before they ever reach a sustainable level. They're bleeding cash from the start and finally fold when the well runs dry. Sorry, but it's true. To me, a business plan only matters when you already have a sustainable business model. Before that, it's all about experimentation.

Try everything. Look for the easiest and quickest way to test new ideas. You'll have a million ideas. I promise. How many times have I had a great idea and been 100 percent convinced I'll be rich by summer? Countless times. Meanwhile, most of my ideas end up falling short. I'm telling you: I've been down this path a thousand times. Are you a failure? Maybe yes, maybe no. Me? Absolutely! No joke. I'm a professional failure! I fail at almost

28

everything I do . . . the first time. But I always get back up. I always learn. I always try again. And eventually, I fail my way to success! And that's precisely why my career has taken off. I'm willing to fail. Not only that, but I think entrepreneurs should fail as often as possible. Why? Because it's evidence that they're trying new things. I have "great" ideas every week and need to give each one a fair shake before moving on to the next. It's the story of my life.

That said, you may be wondering why I titled this chapter "Write a Business Plan." There's a good reason. Having some sort of a plan is nothing more than deciding how you plan to test your next great idea. A plan just forces you to think about that endeavor (testing the idea) in a more structured way. So how can you plan your strategy in a way that doesn't paralyze the process or drive you to the bottle? How about a one-page business plan? Jim Horan wrote a book called *The One-Page Business Plan* (2004) and has since gone on to customize it for a variety of business situations including nonprofits, professional consultants, and financial services. He's also built an army of licensed One-Page Business Plan Consultants. Why has his concept done so well? Because it's simple and it works. Jim does a great job helping entrepreneurs drill down to the core of their market opportunity. He helps them identify the true value proposition behind their product or service as well as the market of people who need what they're selling. And he does it in a straightforward worksheet-based format that's irresistibly clean and simple . . . and it all fits on just one sheet of paper! Visit Amazon and search for "one-page business plan." You'll find a variety of versions of his book. Find the one that matches your business model the best and consider buying a copy. I think it's well worth the investment.

The beauty of Jim's approach is that you can complete a rough draft of your one-page plan in just 20 minutes. So, the next time you have a great idea, take your excitement (new ideas are always exciting, at least for me) and use it to jot down a one-page plan. It'll force you to think through your idea based on a proven formula. By the way, I'm not suggesting you ever need to finish your draft one-page plan. Just use it to structure your approach and then test your idea. If it fails, walk away. No big deal. Move on to the next plan. But if it works, that's the time to map out a strategy in more detail.

Implementation Checklist

- ☐ Don't write a business plan for every idea.
- ☐ Focus on maximizing marketing ideas.
- ☐ Search Amazon for "one-page business plan."
- ☐ Buy the best version for your business.
- ☐ Jot down a one-page plan for every idea.
- ☐ Test every idea to see if it has potential.
- ☐ If it fails, throw it away and move on.
- ☐ If it shows promise, add detail to the plan.
- ☐ Compare notes and ideas with a colleague.

Part Two

Plan Your Internet Presence

Chapter 11

Google Codes and Alerts

Can you hire Google to work for you?

Yes, you can. Better yet, it's free! Obviously, we can all use Google to find the information we need online, but few of us take full advantage of all that Google has to offer. Google provides literally hundreds of online services free of charge. We could never cover them all in one short chapter. But we'll touch on a few basics that can help you squeeze a lot more out of Google than you've probably been doing so far.

First, there are a number of codes you can use to refine your Google searches. You can tell Google which types of websites you want to search for (.com, .net, .edu, .gov, etc.), and you can also specify the types of files you're looking for (pdf, doc, xls, ppt, etc.). How can you leverage these options to your advantage? Here's one example: The next time you're looking for a particular PDF e-book or report, search for a couple relevant keywords along with:

filetype:pdf

Including this code with your keywords will restrict the search to PDF files that include your keywords. This can dramatically accelerate your search and may deliver a number of other related PDF files as well. Every time I do this, I end up finding PDF files I never knew about, but that end up benefiting the cause.

Here's another example of how you can narrow your Google search. The next time you need to make a presentation about a particular topic, search for relevant keywords along with:

filetype:ppt

33

This code will yield PowerPoint presentations that have been posted online and are ready for you to open and learn from. Many of the design elements I use in my PowerPoint presentations were inspired by presentations I found through Google.

You can also use codes to specify the extension of the websites you'd like Google to return in your search. If you want to identify and interact with educational/academic websites with the .edu extension, for example, do a search for your relevant keywords along with:

site:.edu

Yes, you *do* need the dot when referring to website extensions. The above code will restrict the search findings to .edu websites, once again accelerating your search process. Also, a lot of people believe that links from .edu websites are more valuable from a search engine optimization (SEO) perspective, so this code can help you find possible link building opportunities quickly. (We'll talk more about SEO in Chapter 30.)

In addition to these search codes, Google also provides the free Google Alerts tool. Just search for "google alerts" on Google to find it. Using this platform, you can enter keywords (as well as the codes discussed above), and Google will send you e-mails whenever websites matching your search query show up on the Internet. Here are four of the alerts I've signed up for:

conference "call for speakers" −scientific −academic
conference speaker submit proposal −scientific −academic
convention "call for speakers" −scientific −academic
convention speaker submit proposal −scientific −academic

Let's take a closer look at how these Google Alerts work. I'm looking for websites that issue an opportunity for speakers to submit presentation proposals. They generally do so either by posting a "call for speakers" or by including the words "speaker," "submit," and "proposal."

By putting quotation marks around "call for speakers," I am restricting the search to websites that include those three words together, exactly as I have them inside the quotation marks. If I didn't use those quotation marks, the alert would deliver websites with the words "call," "for," and "speakers" in any order, reducing the specificity and relevance for my search intentions. I have also added the words "scientific" and "academic," each with a negative sign in front of it. This format tells Google that I am *not* interested in results that contain these words. There are tons of conferences and conventions that cater to scientific and academic communities. My topic isn't relevant to these audiences so I eliminate those results from my alerts. Every single day, Google e-mails me with search results that are relevant and important to me. I hear about conferences as soon as they're announced. Often, my speaker submission is among the first they receive.

Think about how you can use the same system to fuel your own business. Test different search queries and refine them over time. Before long, Google will be feeding you new leads on a daily basis.

Implementation Checklist

- ☐ Use "filetype:pdf" with your keywords search.
- ☐ Make note of the files you find.
- ☐ Use "site:.edu" with your keywords search.
- ☐ Use "site:.gov" with your keywords search.
- ☐ Make note of the search results.
- ☐ Search for "google alerts" and log in.
- ☐ Create an alert for yourself.
- ☐ Make note of the results you receive.
- ☐ Refine the alert to improve the results.
- ☐ Compare notes and ideas with a colleague.

Chapter 12

Keyword Ideas

Why reinvent the wheel? Look at what your competitors are doing; what you find out about what they're doing right (and wrong) will help you get started.

This chapter (along with the next two) lays the foundation for your website. You might already have a website and that's great. But the vast majority of websites were built without this proper foundation in place. Once we've gone through the process, you'll probably have a very different perspective on what your website needs to do.

Let's dive in. On the Internet, everything boils down to keywords. Everything is indexed according to keywords and a website that's built on efficient targeted keywords has a much better chance of getting found, especially on search engines.

Did you know you can see exactly how your competitors built their own websites? It's true. You can visit any website, right click with your mouse (using Internet Explorer), and select "View Source" from the drop-down menu. Newer versions of Internet Explorer actually have a "View" option right on the toolbar with "Source" listed on the drop-down menu. Viewing the source opens a second window where all the code for that website is displayed. Go try it. If you weren't already aware of this, it'll amaze you. So how can you benefit from viewing a website's source code? Perhaps the biggest opportunity is that you can see exactly which keywords your competitors are targeting. If you're on the homepage of a particular website and you click View Source, you'll notice a few lines of code at the top that start with "meta name." Usually, you'll find one line of code for the site description and one line of code for the keywords being targeted.

Do a search for your ideal keywords and visit the sites that come up first in Google. Because these websites are ranking at the top for the exact keywords you'd like to target as well, it will benefit you to view their source code and see what keywords they are using. Whatever keywords they're targeting are helping them achieve their impressive search engine rankings. This is a great way to start building a list of potential keywords for your own website. Open a Word document and start copying and pasting your competitors' keywords from their websites into your document. It won't take long and you'll have a long list. Go through the keywords and highlight the ones you like. Don't worry about narrowing the list too much. You can have as many keywords as you like. But highlight the ones that relate most closely to your business.

In the next chapter, we'll use the Google keyword tool (mentioned briefly in Chapter 7) to measure the targeting potential of your favorite keywords and give you suggestions for other related keywords as well. For now, just make this big initial list and highlight the keywords you like most. Then put those favorites at the top of the page in a larger font. We'll refine the list later, but it will form the foundation of your web presence.

Once you finalize your keywords list, print it out and post it beside your computer. Every time you write something for your website or blog, look at your list. Use your keywords wherever possible. After a while, it'll become second nature, but at the beginning make sure you have your list nearby and etch those keywords into your mind. For search engines like Google to find your website, your site must offer content about the keywords you're targeting. Your list of keywords tells you exactly what information your website needs to offer. Give the search engines what they're looking for. If you do, you'll be rewarded with better rankings. It's that simple.

Implementation Checklist

- ☐ Identify your ideal keywords and phrases.
- ☐ Search for those keywords on Google.
- ☐ Visit the homepages of the top websites.
- ☐ Right click and select View Source.
- ☐ Copy the keywords listed in the meta tags.
- ☐ Paste the keywords into a Word document.
- ☐ Highlight the keywords you like the most.
- ☐ Print the list with your favorites at the top.
- ☐ Post the list beside your computer screen.
- ☐ Compare notes and ideas with a colleague.

Chapter 13

Keyword Research

Where are the "sitting ducks?"

In Chapter 7, we talked about the publicly accessible Google keyword selector tool and used it to see what search words your potential customers were using. I said it then and I'll say it again: this tool is essential to understanding your market. Keywords are the "key" to identifying opportunities.

When it comes to keywords, the ones you want to find are the *sitting ducks!* What do I mean by that? I'm referring to the keywords that have respectable organic search volume (in other words, they are frequently being searched for) but have almost no competition. Those keywords are what I call sitting ducks. They're just waiting to be targeted! And the Google keyword tool makes them easy to find.

Step 1: Enter one of your primary keywords into the Google keyword tool and sort the list of search results by "competition." By "competition," the Google keyword tool is referring to the pay-per-click (PPC) competition for that particular word or phrase. You may not be interested in doing PPC advertising and that's fine. But competition in the PPC world usually mirrors that of the non-PPC world, so you can extrapolate one from the other.

After the keywords have been resorted, scroll down to the bottom of the list where you'll find the keyword phrases that don't have much competition. The keywords with low competition but good search volume are what we're after.

Step 2: Pick a few phrases that seem to have good search volume but limited competition and write them down. Then search for "Wordtracker keyword tool" on Google and use the free Wordtracker trial to get an estimate of the daily search volume each phrase gets. That'll give you a good idea how many people are actually searching for each phrase. Wordtracker and Google run on different engines and you will find inconsistencies between them. That's okay. The idea is to get as much information as you can and then target the phrases that are the easiest to conquer.

Step 3: Put each keyword phrase with good search volume but limited competition into a standard Google search, using quotation marks around the phrase. Make note of the total number of listings that come up for each. For example, if the Google search results page says "showing 1 to 10 of 238,400 listings" or "about 238,400 listings" (depending on the browser), write down the number 238,400. That gives you a clear idea of how many websites are discussing that precise phrase. The exact number of search results that come up isn't important. The important thing is to *compare* the number of search results for all the different keyword phrases you look up. Some have many thousands of listings while others have far fewer. The keyword phrases with the fewest listings are the easiest to target because they have less competition.

These three simple steps allow you to identify the keyword phrases that are like "sitting ducks," just waiting for some attention. In fact, finding these easy-to-exploit keywords is an extremely sophisticated research process and some companies regularly charge thousands of dollars to conduct the process we just described. I once picked a keyword phrase and got my website on page one of Google search results for that keyword phrase in just 17 days. The phrase was "growth marketing" and it didn't take much for my site to come up first. Why? Because the phrase "growth marketing" had almost no competition. Do I get a ton of traffic from that one phrase? No. But I do get some, each and every month. Can you imagine if you targeted 10 or 20 of these phrases? This stuff works.

Even though effective keyword research can make such a huge difference in terms of your website's search engine ranking, probably 90 percent of companies never do it. Please don't make the common mistake of overlooking this critical step. Efficient keywords are the most important building block for a successful online identity.

One last note: I am generally a big proponent of doing things yourself. That's what this book is all about. And you can definitely handle keyword research. But if you're in doubt at all, it's important enough that I recommend paying a professional to get it right.

Implementation Checklist

☐ Visit the free Google keyword tool.
☐ Search your ideal keywords and phrases.
☐ Sort the results by "competition."
☐ Scroll to the bottom of the list.
☐ Look for low competition but good volume.
☐ Write down the attractive prospects.
☐ Visit the free Wordtracker keyword tool.
☐ Get an estimate of daily search volume.
☐ Google each phrase with quotation marks.
☐ Note the total number of listings for each.
☐ Target best volume and lowest competition.
☐ Hire a professional if you're in doubt.
☐ Compare notes and ideas with a colleague.

Chapter 14

Positioning Statement

What's your positioning statement?

In Chapter 12, I encouraged you to visit your competitors' websites and get keyword ideas from their meta tags. We talked about how the "meta name" source codes of a website list the keywords the site is targeting and give a site description. The previous two chapters were all about the keywords. This chapter is all about the description. The description listed in the meta tags is the website's positioning statement. Every website needs a 15- to 25-word positioning statement. It forms the foundation of the entire website. You need a focus and your positioning statement gives you that focus. In just 15 to 25 words (usually 160 characters or fewer), the statement needs to tell people exactly what you do. Sounds a bit like an elevator pitch, doesn't it? Absolutely. In fact, your positioning statement is just a shorter version of the 75- to 90-word elevator pitch. (Another format—your title tag—is even shorter, at 65 characters or fewer. We'll get to that in a second.)

Where do these statements show up? If you do a Google search for anything, the organic (meaning unsponsored) listings are displayed in the center of the search results page. Every listing includes four lines of text. The top line has the primary title you would click on to visit the website. Below that, you'll find a two-line description telling you what the page is about, and the fourth line provides the actual URL for the page. If you've added a 65-character title tag to your meta tags, this text will show up as the primary title of the listing. If you have a 15- to 25-word positioning statement in your meta tags, this text will appear as the two-line description below the title. And at the bottom, the URL is simply the location where that page resides online.

Most websites don't include title tags or positioning statements in their meta tags. In those cases, Google takes the first 65 characters of the page title for the primary title of the listing and uses the first two lines of page text as the description. If you are not using title tags or positioning statements in your meta tags, you are wasting a huge opportunity. These meta tags speak *directly* to search engines. *Everyone* should take advantage of that! But then again, the fact that most don't enhances the opportunity for those who do! You can always tell which websites include meta tags because they fit perfectly into the space allocated by the search engines. The title tags are 65 characters or fewer and the positioning statements are generally 160 characters or fewer. It's more professional and it helps your rankings.

Get your elevator pitch from Chapter 6 and try to write a shorter version while incorporating the "sitting duck" keyword phrases you identified in Chapter 13. That's the goal. Explain exactly what you do in 15 to 25 words (about 160 characters) while using targeted keyword phrases. Once you're finished, take the next step and summarize it further to a 65-character title tag. *Every* page on your website should have a title tag and a description full of targeted keyword phrases. It's important. If you do this correctly, your chances of ranking high on Google skyrocket. (We'll talk more about this when we discuss SEO in Chapter 29.)

It's worth mentioning that your business focus might change from time to time—there's nothing wrong with that, but make sure you update your website's positioning statement and title tag if necessary. Always remember the important roles that keyword focus and strategic clarity play in your business's visibility on the Internet.

Chapter 26 will introduce a variety of website development platforms. That's where all the keyword research, title tags, and positioning statements come into play. By now you're probably noticing that your competition is overlooking some important steps in creating their Internet presence. Most companies jump right in and start building their website. They only think about how they want the site to look. "I want a blue box here." "I want a beautiful picture there." "I want a fancier font." Meanwhile, they skip the foundation work and wonder why they don't show up on the search engines. Take the steps I've laid out in these past three chapters. You only have to do them once and they'll pay dividends for as long as you have your website. It's worth the time. I promise.

Implementation Checklist

- ☐ Get your elevator pitch (Chapter 6).
- ☐ Get your targeted keywords (Chapter 13).
- ☐ Shorten your pitch to 15 to 25 words.
- ☐ Ensure it is full of targeted keywords.
- ☐ This is your website positioning statement.
- ☐ Shorten it further to just 65 characters.
- ☐ Ensure it contains your primary keywords.
- ☐ This is your homepage title tag.
- ☐ Ensure every web page has a title tag.
- ☐ Ensure every web page has a description.
- ☐ Compare notes and ideas with a colleague.

Chapter 15

Website Sales Function

Is your website making sales?

If your site is like most, probably not. The vast majority of websites do not do a good job converting visitors into happy paying customers. Whether you already have a website or are just starting to think about one, it's important to understand that a website is part of your sales department. Driving traffic to your website, on the other hand, is a function of your marketing department. That's an important distinction. We'll talk about driving traffic later in this book. For now, let's talk about the sales function.

Once your website is discovered by a first-time visitor, the site needs to have a "conversation" with that person. It needs to identify the visitor's problem and how you can solve it. It needs to introduce your products or services and it needs to close the sale. If the site doesn't do these things, it's not doing its job. If you browse around the Internet, you'll find lots of beautiful and well-designed websites, but their good looks don't necessarily mean they convert well. In fact, some of the most basic websites do the best job converting visitors into customers. Why? Because they're so easy to understand.

When planning your website, make sure it answers three simple questions within the first five seconds. Why five seconds? Because that's about how much time you have before a first-time visitor decides whether he or she wants to continue browsing your site or click the "Back" button.

1. **Why am I here?**

Visitors to your site need to understand why they're there. They need to see an explanation of what you do right at the top of the homepage. That's why we worked on your elevator pitch in Chapter 6. That's why we crafted your positioning statement and your title tag. Your title tag should be the lead statement on your homepage, the words in the biggest font. After that, your slightly-longer positioning statement comes next, elaborating on your title tag. And, depending on your website layout, you might even include your entire elevator pitch, fleshing out your Value proposition even further. People need to know what you do. Tell them. They're browsing the Internet for a reason. They're looking for something and it's either on your site or it's not. They need to know if you have what they're looking for and they need to know quickly.

2. Where do I look?

Most websites have far too many options on the homepage. It's confusing. People's eyes glaze over and they lose focus. Studies have confirmed this. The researchers use technology called "eye tracking" to see what people look at when they visit different websites. Too many options destroy your website's "eye flow" and there's no such thing as a confused buyer. The purpose of your homepage is to navigate visitors into the heart of your website. You want your homepage to move visitors to a place where their questions are answered and where they can find what they're looking for. Give your homepage only a small number of buttons that visitors can choose among to navigate deeper into your site. Here are a few superbasic two-button examples:

[I am a man] or [I am a woman]
[I am a physician] or [I am a patient]
[I am an individual] or [I am a business]

These are obvious examples but they make the point. Offer simple navigational buttons that get visitors to the right place. Figure out what the basic distinctions are for your business, the main categories you sell to. Then use your homepage to tell your visitors what you do and navigate them to the right place.

3. What do I do?

Always tell your visitors what to do next. When people visit your website, they are in a submissive position. They are in a receiving mode. They have no control over what they're about to see. You do. That's a huge opportunity that most webmasters never take advantage of. Tell your visitors what to do: "Click here to learn more." "Call us for a free estimate." "Register for our next workshop." "Get a quote today." "Apply now." These are all vitally important instructions. They're all calls to action. Your visitors might be interested or they might not. You'll never know if you don't ask. Demonstrate confidence on your website. Ask for the sale in no uncertain terms. If your website projects confidence, your visitors automatically assume you're more credible. A timid website inspires the opposite assumption. Spend some time thinking about this before you build your website. It's a lot easier to build a new site than to fix an old broken one. Done properly, your website accomplishes the sales job for which it was designed, and that's when the fun starts.

Implementation Checklist

- ☐ Your website is part of your sales department!
- ☐ Generating website traffic is marketing.
- ☐ Think about first-time visitors to your site.
- ☐ Identify exactly what you want them to do.
- ☐ Answer three questions in five seconds.
- ☐ Why am I here? Tell them what you do.
- ☐ Where do I look? Offer a few clear choices.
- ☐ What do I do? Tell them what to do next.
- ☐ Project confidence on your website.
- ☐ Think about this before you start building.
- ☐ Compare notes and ideas with a colleague.

Chapter 16

Website Cornerstone

Focus

What makes a great website?

There are basically three cornerstones to an effective website. These three things encompass everything a website needs. Provide these cornerstones, and your website will excel at catering to both human beings and search engines alike.

1. Focus
2. Depth
3. Value

We'll talk about *Focus* in this chapter. *Depth* is the subject of the next chapter, and *Value* will be discussed in the chapter after that. By structuring your website according to these three cornerstones, you'll be well positioned to capitalize on today's Internet economy.

Focus essentially refers to the keywords on which your website is built. And it's a critically important part of any successful online strategy. Yet, the Focus I'm talking about is counterintuitive for most people and goes against their natural instincts. Follow along with me for a moment. Most people feel like they're restricting themselves if they Focus their website too narrowly. They feel like they're walking away from potential business by pigeonholing themselves with a narrow Focus. This opinion may make sense on some level, but it doesn't help anyone thrive in the online world. An example may help illustrate why.

Let's assume you're a financial advisor who's trying to sell annuities, life insurance, and estate planning services. If you built your website to present a balance among those three services, Google would interpret your website to be roughly 33 percent about each topic. If someone did a Google search for life insurance, what do you think the search engine would do? If another website was 100 percent devoted to life insurance, do you think that site would come up higher than yours? All other things being equal, probably. The search engines look for density of unique relevant content as defined by the words used in the search query and related words. If only 33 percent of your website relates to the words used in the search query, your website comes up lower in the search results than other websites that are more exclusively devoted to that topic. That's an oversimplification, but you get the point.

Now, if your site came up on page 7 of the Google search results for three different topics, do you think you'd get any traffic from Google? No. Absolutely not. Very few people ever get past the second or third page of search results. On the other hand, if you came up on page 1 or 2 for *one* topic, do you think you'd get traffic as a result? The answer is *yes*. Back in Chapter 2, we reviewed the common Internet saying, "go an inch wide and a mile deep." That means you're better off selecting a narrow topic and then building massive content around that topic. We'll talk about the "massive" part (*Depth*) in the next chapter, but for now we'll look at your narrow *Focus,* which is critical.

Let's get back to our example. If you specialized only in life insurance and if you managed to rank on page one for some related keyword phrases, you would definitely start getting traffic from Google. Once they arrive on your website, do you think it would be possible to cross-sell them your other services such as annuities and estate planning later on?

Your specialty is simply intended to get you noticed online. You can even devote a small part of your website to the other services you offer; just make sure you keep the overwhelming focus on your primary specialty. I once built a website for a bank. The entire site was devoted to its real estate division, which specialized in 1031 exchanges (1031 exchanges are a particular type of real estate transaction designed for investment properties). In other words, the site was extremely focused and had 94 pages of content all about that specific topic. By comparison, my own blog (called Tactical Execution) had more than 500 pages of content but it covered a wide variety of different topics. Amazingly, the bank's website got more than twice as many visitors from Google as my blog did. You would think the volume of my content would win. Nope. The smaller site's *Focus* gave that site the overwhelming advantage in the battle for search engine results.

Obviously, a website with both content *and* Focus offers the best alternative, but the comparison of the bank's website to my own illustrates the point. *Focus* is critically important for a successful website. Think about your business. Think about your expertise and select an area where you can become a true authority. Use the keyword research tools we discussed in Chapter 13 to identify the most efficient keyword phrases and then build your website around that narrow focus. The next chapter is all about *Depth* and it deals precisely with the volume of content on your website. It's the second cornerstone of an effective website.

Implementation Checklist

- ☐ Select one focused area in which to specialize.
- ☐ Review your targeted keyword phrases.
- ☐ Build your website as focused as possible.
- ☐ Resist the instinct to cover everything.
- ☐ Ensure one keyword phrase dominates.
- ☐ Cross-sell other products or services later.
- ☐ Compare notes and ideas with a colleague.

Chapter 17

Website Cornerstone
Depth

What's the easiest way to accumulate massive content for your website?

That's not an easy question to answer but we'll look at a few ideas in a second. First, let's get back to the three cornerstones of an effective website and review our progress. The three cornerstones are:

1. Focus
2. Depth
3. Value

In Chapter 16, we discussed *Focus* and the importance of selecting one specialty to form the foundation of your online identity. In this chapter, we'll move on to the second cornerstone: *Depth*.

When someone puts a few keywords into a search query, the search engines look out into the Internet and deliver websites that have a large quantity of unique relevant content containing the keywords entered along with words that are related to the keywords entered. Incidentally, if you're curious how the search engines know what words are related to the keywords entered, they simply look into the search history to see what other words were commonly included in searches that contained the same keywords being searched for by the current user.

Let's say someone searches for the word "mortgage." The search engines quickly see that previous searchers also included the words "refinance" and "purchase," for example, when doing searches for "mortgage." As a result, the search engines know "mortgage," "refinance," and "purchase" are all related words. Bottom line: The more content you have on your website about those keywords, the more likely you are to come up high on the search engine's results page.

So how do you accumulate all this content? That depends on whether or not you like to write and produce content.

If you enjoy writing content, let me offer a word of advice: Write an outline of all the topics you could cover before you start typing. The reason for this is simple. Without an outline, all the knowledge in your head is interrelated. If you just start writing, you'll peripherally mention too many different things too quickly. After just three or four posts, you'll run out of things to say. If, on the other hand, you write an outline first, you'll force your mind to organize the knowledge you have and structure it into a series of specific topics. In fact, you'll probably find yourself subdividing topics into more and more minute details you could cover. I did this once myself. Within an hour or two, I had a list of almost 60 topics I could cover. After that, whenever I had some extra time, I'd pull out my list, select a topic to write about, and then cross it off my list.

If you hate writing or find that you just don't have that much to say, I offer two suggestions. First, go to a website like EzineArticles.com (we talked about this in Chapter 2) and do some searches for your favorite keywords. You'll quickly find hundreds or even thousands of articles about those keywords. You can use these articles as inspiration for your own writing. They can give you a ton of ideas quickly.

You can also post these articles directly on your own website as long as you include the Author Resource Box, linking back to the author's website. That's the way it works. That's what those authors are looking for. They'll be thrilled with the added exposure. If you decide to publish other people's articles on your own website, don't expect the articles to improve your rankings with Google. Search engines look for duplicate content when indexing the Internet, so your reproduced articles won't give you a better position on the search results page. They only benefit you in terms of the extra information they allow you to offer your visitors.

My second suggestion is to get others to create content on your behalf. I have two clients who accept articles written by their customers for inclusion on their respective blogs. Both parties win. The customers get a chance to demonstrate their expertise in front of a new audience and my clients get unique relevant content for their websites. You can also hire young writers to blog on your behalf. This cutting-edge marketing strategy has taken no-name companies to prominence in record time. You could hire a few

23-year-old college graduates to write for your blog and have lots of content quickly. At the beginning, pay them per post. In time, pay your bloggers bonuses according to the amount of traffic their posts receive and the amount of time their visitors spend on the site. These things are easy to track using tools like Google Analytics (discussed in Chapter 33).

One way or another, if you want your website to get high rankings by the search engines, you need to build massive unique relevant content around your narrow focus. Think about which strategy works for you and start accumulating content today. One last note: never take content away. Only add. Always add. Over time, you want your website to grow and grow. That's the beauty of blogs—just keep adding more. (We'll talk more about blogs starting in Chapter 26.)

Implementation Checklist

- ☐ Create an outline of topics you can cover.
- ☐ Subdivide your topics as much as possible.
- ☐ Write about a topic when you have time.
- ☐ Visit EzineArticles.com to get ideas.
- ☐ Consider publishing other people's articles.
- ☐ Invite your clients to contribute content.
- ☐ Consider hiring people to write content.
- ☐ Pay bonuses for high-traffic posts.
- ☐ Never remove content. Always add more.
- ☐ Compare notes and ideas with a colleague.

Chapter 18

Website Cornerstone

Value

Why would your website visitors come back to your site again and again?

The answer is *Value*. If visitors get value from your website, they'll come back a second time and a third. More important, they'll tell their friends about your site. That endorsement is worth far more than any advertising you might be doing! Before we get into the details, let's get back to the three cornerstones of an effective website and review our progress.

1. Focus
2. Depth
3. Value

In Chapter 16, we discussed *Focus* and the importance of selecting one specialty as the foundation for your online identity. In Chapter 17, we discussed *Depth* and how to accumulate massive content on your website. In this chapter, we'll conclude this topic with a discussion about *Value*. Generally speaking, *Value* comes in one of the following three forms:

1. Updated content
2. Value items
3. Resource tools

Updated content refers to those pieces of data that change over time and can be updated on your website. Interest rates, stock market quotes, real estate values, horoscopes, news feeds, blog posts, podcasts, and birthday reminders are all examples of content that can be updated. If a website had one of these examples, you could visit the same site on different days and get different content each time. Obviously, the type of content you could display on your website will depend on your field, but I encourage you to think about things you can post on your website that will update automatically. These days, a lot of web platforms offer fancy "widgets" you can add to your website quickly and easily. In this context, widgets are little pieces of code you can copy and paste onto your website, adding functionality for your visitors. The Facebook "Like" button is a great example. Visit widgetbox.com and search for your favorite keywords to find widgets in your field. That way, you could incorporate updating content on your website without having to update it yourself. Blogs are an excellent example of updating content as well, and the best part is that you're in complete control over the content you're offering. Is it more work than a widget? Yes. But the possible upside is bigger as well. Blogs are a powerful tool in modern marketing and you might want to consider including one in your marketing strategy. (We'll talk more about that starting in Chapter 26.)

Value items include things of significance people can get on your website. It might be a report about your field. It might be a few instructional videos. It might be a series of educational articles or a PDF document with important definitions in your business. From a slightly more sophisticated perspective, it could be a Facebook application. It could be a mobile phone application. It could be a WordPress theme or a unique ringtone. Of course, these examples involve some actual coding, but the marketing potential is huge and many companies are building their audiences by offering these sophisticated Value items to website visitors.

Resource tools include any Web-based functionality that helps you do something. As you might imagine, there's a wide variety of examples of these kinds of tools. At the simplest level, resource tools might include mortgage payment calculators and calorie counters. On the more sophisticated end, these tools could include any of the web platforms designed to help you manage your life. Online banking platforms come to mind, along with websites such as OpenTable.com, EverNote.com, and BaseCampHQ.com. Again, these last examples all involve extensive coding to create. But that doesn't mean you can't offer your audience tools they can use. In many cases, you can use widgets hosted by other platforms and incorporate those into your website. Again, visit widgetbox.com and do a search for your favorite keywords. You might be surprised how many resource tools are available, and most of them are absolutely free.

Updated content, value items, and resource tools all represent things you can offer to bring visitors back to your website again and again. Get creative with the ideas we've discussed here and develop your own proprietary blend of value to provide your audience. It all helps to build your traffic and solidify your position as an authority in your field.

Focus, Depth, and *Value* are the cornerstones of an effective website. The last three chapters dealt with each in turn. Keep these concepts in mind as you build out your online identity; they are important not just to your website but to your Internet activities in general. Focus, Depth, and Value will provide enduring guideposts for your journey.

Implementation Checklist

- ☐ Consider updated content in your field.
- ☐ Think about information you could share.
- ☐ Visit widgetbox.com to look for examples.
- ☐ Consider Value items you could provide.
- ☐ Allocate time to create these Value items.
- ☐ Consider resource tools you could offer.
- ☐ Incorporate functionality on your website.
- ☐ Let Focus, Depth, and Value define your site.
- ☐ Compare notes and ideas with a colleague.

Chapter 19

Website Conversation

What do you want your website visitors to learn about you?

Whenever someone stumbles upon your website, a "conversation" takes place. In fact, even before the conversation starts, there's a first impression, just like in the offline world. Consider these dynamics when building your website.

Let's start with the first impression. This relates to the three important questions we covered in Chapter 15. Your website needs to answer the first question, Why am I here?, right away. Your visitors need to find out if your website has what they are looking for . . . or not.

The way to do that is to put your positioning statement front and center on your homepage and then offer a few clear choices so visitors can navigate to an area of the website that addresses their needs. If they click on one of those choices, they're telling you that they still believe your website has what they are looking for. That's great news! This is where the conversation starts taking shape. As visitors navigate through your website, they learn things about you. They learn what you do and what you offer. You have control over what they learn, and in what order. Yet, few business owners take advantage of that opportunity.

Whether you already have a website or not, take some time to write down a series of statements that you'd like your website visitors to learn about you. Don't worry which are the most important or what order the statements should be in. Just write them down. Try to come up with at least 10 statements that you want your website visitors to think about when they think about you. Here are some examples:

1. Patrick Schwerdtfeger offers tested marketing strategies for small businesses.

2. Patrick Schwerdtfeger has many useful free resources available on his website.

3. Patrick Schwerdtfeger provides solutions that can help entrepreneurs build their businesses.

You get the idea. Allocate some time and do the exercise. Make a list first and then put your statements in a logical order second. What do you want visitors to learn first? Second? Third? These statements will form the basis for the various pages that navigate visitors through your website.

At some point in their journey through your site, the next thing your visitors learn might depend on who they are. In other words, there may be a fork in the road into your site. Chapter 15 discussed how your homepage should navigate your visitors into the heart of your site, to a location that addresses their needs. Often, your secondary pages do the same thing, segmenting your visitors even further. Depending on the selections they make, your visitors might end up in a dozen different locations on your site. Each page needs to communicate a clear message to the visitor. As the pages divide visitors according to their selections, so too must your website address their increasingly qualified needs. A conversation is taking place and you can script your side of it the same way some companies use scripts for customer service phone calls.

Most websites are like unkempt fields completely overgrown with weeds and bushes; there's stuff everywhere with no real rhyme or reason. Chop a path through that field. That's essentially what you're doing when you define what information to present to your visitors, and choose where to present it. You're building a path for your visitors to walk on. Along the way, you can decide what they see and what they learn. You can even put some bread crumbs along the way, slowly guiding them to the purchase page. A well-thought-out conversation with your visitors encourages interaction and builds trust. Interaction = trust. The more you can get your visitors to interact with your website, the more they'll trust you as a provider. I know this might sound esoteric but the concept is important. You have complete control over your website. You control what's on the homepage and you control what's on all the other pages as well. Take advantage of that opportunity! Figure out what you want your visitors to learn and then build a path for them to walk on. If you do, it will dramatically improve the conversion rate your website delivers.

Implementation Checklist

- ☐ Your website should make sales!
- ☐ Decide what your visitors should learn.
- ☐ Plan the conversation your website has.
- ☐ Qualify your website visitors on each page.
- ☐ Always craft your message to the visitor.
- ☐ Build a "path" for your visitors to walk on.
- ☐ Encourage interaction along the way.
- ☐ Compare notes and ideas with a colleague.

Chapter 20

Expand the Frame

How do you take your business to the next level?

In this chapter, we borrow some concepts from "social dynamics" theory to dramatically expand the frame of your business. Let me start with a quick story. A past client has a business selling wine jelly. Yes, that's right. Wine jelly. Apparently, it tastes really good. But that's not the point. Before we met, his website had products ranging in price from $4 to $28. They included different sized jars and one package deal with four large jars. Now, imagine what you might think if you were to stumble upon his website.

If it were me, I would picture a retail shelf vendor and nothing more. I would picture a few jars with a particular label sitting there on the shelf beside dozens of competitive products. Nothing would jump out at me. And that's precisely the problem. He was a retail shelf vendor and nothing more. We needed to expand the frame. To do this, we introduced a once-annual three-day retreat in the Napa Valley wine country, including an extensive tour of a winery on one day, an afternoon workshop on a second day (teaching participants how to make wine jelly in their own homes), and three gourmet meals per day, each featuring wine jelly in one fashion or another. The price for the retreat was $3,995 and he featured it on his homepage. Now, imagine once again what you would think if you were to discover this website.

In the first case, you found a retail shelf vendor selling little jars of jelly. In the second scenario, you found a parallel universe that you never knew existed: a world full of romance, passion, and good food. You discovered a world you'd never seen before, a potential hobby, and a rich addition to your life. It's a totally different "frame," a totally different experience. Keep in mind: Nobody needs to buy the retreat package, at least not at the beginning. The important thing is that the package is there on the home-page, offering a unique experience.

Remember that when someone clicks onto your website, they are in the submissive position. They are in a receiving mode. They have absolutely no control over what they are about to see. You do. We talked about this in Chapter 19. You control everything that visitors to your site see. You control the frame. And you can expand the frame.

That's a huge opportunity that few businesses take advantage of. You can present a small timid frame with your little product or service available for sale. Or you can present a huge overwhelming presence full of opportunities to change people's lives. It's your choice. Think bigger. Expand the frame of your business. Think about the personal objectives of your prospective customers. They are people. They have their own goals and passions. Think of ways to let them pursue their own objectives within the context of your business. Cater to their innermost desires. Cater to their human side. Cater to their emotions.

Don't ever underestimate the passion of your customers. Some of them are more passionate about your topic than *you* are! They might not all buy what you're offering. That's okay. But some will. Trust me. Some will. You'll see. Some will engage and see your business as a way for them to improve their own lives. Cater to *them*! Build your business for them. They have friends. And if your business is improving their lives, you can bet they'll be telling their friends. And some of your other less-passionate customers might just get a bit jealous and engage more themselves.

Another great example is what Barack Obama did during his 2008 campaign. I don't care if you like his politics or not. That's not important here. But during his campaign, he created a website that allowed supporters to get involved in an incredibly productive way. They could have "friends," create a "neighborhood," attend events, and even organize their own events. They could start their own blog right on his platform to share campaign experiences with friends, which more than 60,000 people did! With his campaign website, Barack Obama expanded the frame. He gave his supporters an opportunity to achieve their own objectives *within* his campaign. Some people wanted to become "big wigs" in his campaign and his platform gave them a way to do it. Others wanted to organize local events. His website gave them the tools. Some wanted to encourage others to donate money. His website gave them a way to match funds for new donors. Others just wanted to meet people with similar political interests and Barack Obama's website provided a social network for his supporters to meet and connect with each other.

There's a moral to these stories. Think bigger. Redefine what you do. Incorporate your customers' personal objectives into your business model. They'll be happier and so will you. Present an overwhelming online identity and watch your customer interactions change forever! As an exercise, think about your most expensive product or service offering. How much does it cost? Take that price and multiply it by 20. Sell something for *that* price! So if your most expensive product is $100, create something to sell for $2,000. If your most expensive service package is $1,000, create a new package for $20,000. Don't worry about who's going to buy it. That's not the point. The point is to explode your vision of your own business and then reflect that vision to people who find you. Even if nobody ever buys the new product or service, its mere existence will improve the perceptions people have of your business. Don't be a retail shelf vendor. Be more than that. Be a parallel universe! Provide your customers and prospects with a whole new world. Show them the lifestyle your product or service supports. Show them the glamour, the passion, and the romance. That's what gets people to buy!

Implementation Checklist

- [ ] Consider your customers' personal lives.
- [ ] List their passions and personal objectives.
- [ ] Brainstorm ways to cater to that list.
- [ ] Think bigger about your business model.
- [ ] Offer products with higher price points.
- [ ] Don't worry if people buy them or not.
- [ ] Promote your most extravagant product.
- [ ] See who responds and solicit feedback.
- [ ] Calibrate your product offerings.
- [ ] Present an overwhelming online identity.
- [ ] Offer your product menu with confidence.
- [ ] Expand the frame of your business!
- [ ] Compare notes and ideas with a colleague.

Chapter 21

Categorize Your Content

What should you give away? What should you charge money for?

Marketing in the twenty-first century is all about demonstrating your expertise and providing value *before* asking for the sale. It's about offering your audience a sample of your brilliance so they can experience your value. So what information do you have to give away for free? The answer to that question involves categorizing your content; it's the subject of this chapter and one of the most important concepts in this book

Before we get started, we have to define "content." I'm talking about your expertise. I'm talking about your knowledge. I'm talking about the things you know that other people *want* to know.

If you don't already have a particular area of expertise, you need to get one. You need to look out into the universe and pick your niche—pick the thing you're going to be an expert in. Even if you sell a product, you can be an expert in the uses of that product or the technology behind that product. Whatever you do, you need to stake your claim and become an authority on your topic. We discussed this in Chapter 2. Once you start accumulating content, break it down into three categories: beginner, intermediate, and advanced. Every time you acquire new content, think of these categories and add your new knowledge to the appropriate category.

Here's the plan: In your effort to demonstrate your expertise and build trust with your audience, you're going to give the beginner content away for free. You can use it to build your website, write blog posts, publish articles, create podcasts, or record YouTube videos. Give away the intermediate content as well but collect information about your audience in exchange for it. For example, you could ask for names and e-mail addresses in exchange for a PDF white paper or a special report. You could also get your audience to fill out a brief survey to receive the content. Either way, you're using the intermediate content as a way of learning more about your audience. This information plays an important role in your future marketing strategies.

The advanced content is where you make some money. This is where you finally earn a profit. You could deliver this advanced content in the form of consulting jobs. You could create information products (like a big e-book or a bunch of CDs or DVDs) and sell them online. You could write a book or conduct training workshops. Whatever you choose, when you sell your advanced content is when you can finally put some cash in your pocket.

Keep in mind that the advanced content could simply be the practical application of the intermediate content. A lot of people have access to great information, but they don't understand how to take action. That means your advanced content could involve detailed instructions for using your intermediate content.

Get started by listing all the specific little topics you could address. Break up your list by putting each topic into the appropriate category: beginner, intermediate, or advanced. Pretend you're a teacher and treat your content as a series of lessons. That makes it easier to put the information into categories. It's very important to get this concept right. Your Internet marketing efforts depend on a content-rich website and strategic sampling of your expertise across the web. The next three chapters go into each category in more detail and provide some specific examples.

Implementation Checklist

- ☐ Pretend you're a teacher.
- ☐ Think about all the lessons you could offer.
- ☐ Create a detailed list of all these lessons.
- ☐ Add to the list any time you think of more.
- ☐ Identify all the beginner lessons (topics).
- ☐ Identify all the intermediate lessons.
- ☐ Identify all the advanced lessons.
- ☐ Split your total list into three categories.
- ☐ Always think in terms of these categories.
- ☐ Compare notes and ideas with a colleague.

Chapter 22

Beginner Content = Trust

How can you leverage your content?

If you're smart about this, you can create your content once . . . *and repurpose it seven different ways!* You can literally flood the Internet with your expertise and work *less* than your competition. In Chapter 21, we talked about categorizing your content into beginner, intermediate, and advanced. The idea was to give the beginner content away to demonstrate your expertise and build trust with your audience. Your website or blog is the perfect place for some of that beginner content. Get the list of "lessons" you put together and look through your beginner and intermediate topics. Let's start with the beginner topics. (We'll get to the intermediate category in Chapter 23.)

Take each beginner lesson and write an article about it. Always make sure your articles are at least 500 words long. If you write an article that's longer than 1,500 words, break it into two separate articles. Are you ready? We'll be using your articles in seven different ways, maximizing the bang you get for your buck. If you don't have your website built yet, don't worry. The important thing is to realize how your content can be repurposed on the Internet. Knowing this process will help you deploy your online strategy once you start building.

First, publish your article as a post on your blog. Easy enough.

Second, bookmark your new blog post on a few of the large social bookmarking sites like Digg, Delicious, Reddit, and StumbleUpon. (We'll describe how to do this in Chapter 45.)

Third, visit BlogCarnival.com and submit your new blog post to a bunch of upcoming blog carnivals. (We'll explain this process in Chapter 43.)

Fourth, modify your article slightly and publish it on EzineArticles.com and some of the other article directories on the Internet. You could even use a distribution platform like iSnare.com to get it on hundreds of sites within a few days. (We'll talk about this in Chapter 52.)

Fifth, summarize your article into a punchy bullet-point PDF file; make sure the PDF includes plenty of links to your website. Upload your new PDF to the many free e-book directories such as ebookdirectory.com or ebook2u.com. Yes, it's true. There are dozens of e-book directories and their visitors are searching for information. They can find your information . . . but only if you upload it.

Sixth, read your article into a microphone and record it. Now you have a podcast that you can register on iTunes and dozens of "podcast directories." (We'll discuss podcasting in detail in Chapter 51.)

Seventh, get a Flip digital video recorder (about $200) and record yourself as you explain the topic you wrote about in your article. Don't worry. It doesn't have to be fancy. Just speak about the concept as if you were explaining it to a friend. Once you're done, add your website address to the video and upload it to YouTube.

These seven effective ways to get your beginner content out into the world will cost you next to nothing (except perhaps if you need to invest in the Flip recorder). Yet very few people take advantage of these opportunities to spread their message across the Internet. By following these steps, you can take one piece of beginner content—*one* lesson—and use it in seven different formats, populating multiple platforms with your expertise. This is powerful stuff. It's extremely efficient and caters to the different ways people use the Internet.

Don't make this more difficult than it needs to be. Most people think they need to create new content for every platform. No way! That's too much work. You could write one lesson every week or two and end up with a massive online identity within a few months. This chapter offers one of the most powerful strategies you could imagine, but most people reading it won't follow the advice. If you could commit to just one thing, commit to this. If you follow these seven steps, you'll spend less time and get better results than 99 percent of your competition.

Implementation Checklist

- ☐ Pick a topic and write a 500-word article.
- ☐ Publish your article as a post on your blog.
- ☐ Submit your article to the social bookmarking sites.
- ☐ Submit your article to upcoming blog carnivals.
- ☐ Modify and publish your article on article directories.
- ☐ Make your article into a punchy how-to PDF e-book.
- ☐ Upload your article to the free e-book directories.
- ☐ Read your article into a microphone and save as MP3.
- ☐ Register your MP3 file as a podcast on iTunes.
- ☐ Buy a Flip recorder or a camcorder.
- ☐ Record yourself talking about the topic.
- ☐ Add your website address to the video.
- ☐ Upload the video to YouTube.
- ☐ Compare notes and ideas with a colleague.

Chapter 23

Intermediate Content = List

E-mail List → Audience → Influence → Revenue

We touched on e-mail distribution lists back in Chapter 9. In that chapter, we identified three types of e-mail lists:

1. Your own list.
2. Joint venture lists.
3. E-mail distribution lists.

In this chapter, we'll talk about how you can use your intermediate content to develop your own e-mail list. Obviously, one of the most valuable pieces of information you can get from people is their e-mail address. Once you have that, you can stay in touch with them far into the future. Chapter 22 showed you how to leverage your beginner content by using it in seven different ways on different platforms and catering to different audiences in different places. That's a great lesson in how to get more exposure with less work. But there's one thing we haven't discussed yet and it's just as important as leveraging your content. Wherever you offer your free beginner content, you *must* tell your audience what else you offer (your intermediate and advanced content) and include a call to action so they know how to get it. Your beginner content demonstrates your expertise, but your intermediate content is where your audience starts to interact with you. Your intermediate content is the beginning of your sales funnel.

Let's say you have a 17-page white paper as your intermediate content. Maybe it reveals new trends in your industry. Perhaps it lists the top tactics to find new clients, grow revenues, or reduce costs. One great idea is to do a survey and then compile the results into a report. At the bottom of your blog post, you should instruct your readers to click a link to receive the report. When publishing your articles at the various article directories, use the Author Resource Box to tell people about the report and provide a link. When uploading a free e-book, make sure it has links to the report. When you record your podcast and make your YouTube video, be sure to mention the report and tell your listeners and viewers where to get it.

All of your beginner content should point to your intermediate content. You're building a sales funnel. You're leading your prospects down a path. First, you tease them with some great complimentary information—whet their appetite. Then, you entice them with more goodies—more valuable incentives—to take action and interact with you.

Soon, we'll be inviting them to spend money, but not yet. We still need to build our list. We want your audience to be *so* impressed that spending money with you is a complete no-brainer. We'll get to that in the next chapter. For now, the important thing to remember is that at this stage you are distributing your content as part of an exchange. The people who take the next step need to give you their e-mail address (or perhaps their cell phone number for text message campaigns) before they get the promised intermediate content, and an e-mail autoresponder makes that easy to do.

What's an autoresponder? It's a platform that can manage your e-mail marketing efforts. You can upload prewritten e-mails that go out automatically when someone subscribes. The platform can also manage unsubscribe requests when people want to leave the list, all while maintaining the database of e-mail addresses in a secure location. An autoresponder is absolutely essential to modern marketing. Three of my favorite providers are Constant Contact, Infusionsoft, and aWeber. Some of you may already know about my fondness for these platforms. In fact, this book began as a free e-mail course on my Tactical Execution website. Those who subscribed got one e-mail each week for a year, and it was all done automatically. I didn't have to do a thing. The platform automatically sent out the e-mails according to a predetermined time-lapse (one e-mail per week) schedule.

Using an autoresponder, you can quickly create a simple sign-up form and put it on your website. Believe me: it's easy to do! Then, you can write the first e-mail people receive when they sign up. You can also upload a PDF file and have the autoresponder attach the PDF to the e-mail. That means it can deliver a report or white paper (or whatever) all without you having to lift a finger.

What does this mean? It means you need to create your intermediate content first and then create a page on your website where people can enter their e-mail address to receive the content. (And don't forget: You need to include a call to action with every piece of beginner content you publish.) Whether you're using Constant Contact or aWeber or some other autoresponder, you can usually create as many lists as you want. If you already have an autoresponder set up, don't worry. Just create a separate list and a separate sign-up form and you'll start building a second list. Some people will sign up for one or the other. Some will sign up for both. I have six different sign-up forms on my websites, feeding six different lists. And when I send out a broadcast e-mail to all my lists at the same time, the platform automatically ensures nobody gets duplicate e-mails.

By the way, your intermediate content could also be a complimentary one-hour consultation or a property assessment or a portfolio analysis or a website critique or virtually anything. Take some time to think about your intermediate content. Start structuring it in such a way that makes it possible for you to offer the content to your prospects in return for their e-mail address. What are you really doing? You're qualifying your prospects, that's what! This is Sales 101. The people who request your intermediate content are demonstrating their interest in your expertise. They are demonstrating their trust in your knowledge. In Chapter 24, we'll give them something to buy!

Implementation Checklist

- ☐ Decide what your intermediate content is.
- ☐ Make sure it's built and ready for delivery.
- ☐ Give it away for free to gather information.
- ☐ Select an e-mail autoresponder provider.
- ☐ Create a sign-up form on their platform.
- ☐ Build a page on your website with the offer.
- ☐ Embed the sign-up form on your website.
- ☐ Sign up yourself to test the process.
- ☐ Describe your offer with a call to action.
- ☐ Include it with all your beginner content.
- ☐ Compare notes and ideas with a colleague.

Chapter 24

Advanced Content = Revenue

Who's ready to make some money?!?

The past two chapters were about building a sales funnel with your beginner and intermediate content. We've been leaving bread crumbs on the path, letting people sample your expertise and pulling them through the sales funnel by enticing them along the way. And in return for this value, you've captured their e-mail address. These are now warm prospects. They already know who you are. The whole point is to qualify your prospects. At each stage, you're offering more value. Those who are no longer interested drop off, but those who want more will stay with you. It's a sales funnel. You're providing value and building trust. Now, you have to sell them something!

Your advanced content can take a lot of different forms. Perhaps the final sales proposition is just a product and the beginner and intermediate content was only intended to show your knowledge of that product. Perhaps it's your services as a mortgage broker, chiropractor, financial advisor, massage therapist, or insurance agent. Maybe it's a big information product or a membership program or an intensive three-day workshop. Are you curious what mine is? My advanced content is my speaking engagements. That's what I'm looking for. That's my passion. I speak about modern entrepreneurship, online branding, and the social media revolution. I speak about our changing economy and my message is one of empowerment and opportunity. You'll find me at www.PatrickSchwerdtfeger.com.

Think about your own advanced content. What exactly are you selling? What problem are you solving? What pain are you alleviating? Start a list of all the different things you could offer that fall into the advanced content category. Don't wait. You have to know where you're going. You have to know where you're leading your prospects. In earlier chapters, we discussed planning your website. Chapter 15 was all about knowing precisely what you want your website visitors to do. You want to answer their question, Why am I here? Most webmasters can't answer that simple question for their visitors. They don't have a clear idea of what they want their website visitors to do.

Not only do you need that clarity for the development of your website but you need it for your content categories and your revenue model as well. Define exactly what your advanced content is and how you plan to package it for your audience. For example, I don't recommend charging for your expertise by the hour. Instead, package a solution and charge a fee that reflects the value being delivered. Refer back to Chapter 20 about "expanding the frame." It was about having a broader view of your business and offering different products at different price points to cater to the different objectives and passions of your audience. That all applies here too.

When structuring your advanced content solutions, be sure to include something very inexpensive—maybe just $10—and other things that are very extravagant and expensive—maybe $4,000 or more. Expand the frame. Broaden your perspective. Create a menu of products or services that spans far and wide! Here's your opportunity to build a revenue model. Here's your opportunity to make some money. Don't let it slip through your fingers. You've earned it! You've demonstrated your expertise. You've provided value. You've built trust. Now, you have to start earning some money. This is where the planning all comes together. It's like building a house. You have to pour the concrete first. It takes time and rarely offers much visible progress from a distance. But once the foundation is built, the framers come in and the house goes up quickly.

We're at the framing stage. This is where you step out and ask your audience to buy something. This is often the hardest part because you have to believe in yourself first. That confidence will build as you accumulate more e-mail subscribers, but it takes time. It takes patience. This section of the book is still about planning your Internet presence but most of the rest of the book is all about infrastructure, traffic, and revenue. All of that will contribute to your confidence too.

Always remember this: Even if you still feel a bit shaky with your expertise, never underestimate the passion of your prospects. Never underestimate the confidence they already have in you. Never underestimate the need they have for your expertise. Some of the people in your audience already want to take action. They want to move forward. They believe in you.

They believe you can solve their problem. If you don't give them a way to take action, you are doing them a disservice. Don't wait for 100 percent of your audience to be ready to buy. Some of them are ready now. Some of them are ready today. Give them what they want and worry about the others later. Categorize your content. Package your value. And go make some money!

Implementation Checklist

- [ ] Clarify your advanced content solutions.
- [ ] Determine price based on value delivered.
- [ ] Tell your audience about your solutions.
- [ ] Create a broad product or service menu.
- [ ] Offer both simple and extravagant solutions.
- [ ] Never underestimate your audience.
- [ ] Some of them are ready to take action.
- [ ] Cater to your most passionate prospects.
- [ ] Gain confidence from your e-mail list.
- [ ] Work through the rest of this book!
- [ ] Compare notes and ideas with a colleague.

Chapter 25

Killer Sales Copy

Have you heard about the motivating sales sequence?

I haven't used that phrase so far in this book, but we did use the concept right at the beginning. We used it when we discussed your elevator pitch in Chapter 6. The motivating sales sequence is a basic sales process. It's a way of telling someone about something . . . but it's a convincing way! With your elevator pitch, you were telling people about *you*, but you can use the same process to tell them about your product or service. This chapter is about using the motivating sales sequence to write effective sales copy for your website. I'm talking about the product and service descriptions that are designed to convince readers to *buy*. Effective sales copy equals higher conversion rates. That means a higher percentage of your website visitors actually purchase your product or service. (That's a good thing.)

The motivating sales sequence has seven specific steps. Each step gives the reader different information, but they're all essential; the order of the steps is critically important as well. Follow along:

Step 1: Get Their Attention

Start with something amazing, shocking, or provocative. Reference an incredible statistic. Make a controversial statement. Ask a provocative question. The opening sentences need to jolt your readers to attention.

Step 2: Identify the Problem or Need

Once you have their attention, you need to identify the problem and the pain your product or service alleviates. People have lots of problems but

73

they're only willing to spend money when the problem gives them some *pain*.

Step 3: Position Your Product as the Solution

Explain how your product solves the problem and alleviates the pain. Focus on the benefits, not the features. Better yet, describe the emotions— the emotions of the *pain* and the way your customers will feel when the pain is gone.

Step 4: Differentiate Yourself from the Competition

How are you different? What makes you better? This is where you present your value proposition (Chapter 5). Some people refer to this as your unique selling proposition (USP). It explains why your product or service is different and better than all the other options.

Step 5: Establish Credibility and Build Value

Explain why your product is worth more than the price you're charging. Describe your experience. Talk about your guarantees. Tell them how much more the competition's products cost. Describe all the bonuses your customers will get when they purchase your product.

Step 6: Provide Proof (Statistics and Testimonials)

Answer the instinctive question, "Why should I believe you?" Here's where you pull out the statistics. Have you won any awards? Do you have any special credentials? What about testimonials? Testimonials are extremely effective at building trust with your audience, especially if you include photos, audio, or video.

Step 7: Close with a Call to Action

This is the most important step. Ask for the sale. Be specific. Explain exactly what you want the reader to do. Missing this one step cuts your conversion in half. The people who are interested want to know how to take action. Don't deny them that opportunity.

And Finally, Give Them Something to *Buy*!

By now it should be clear what this process is designed to do. It's a way to walk people through a logical mental progression that offers your product as the best possible alternative for their situation. These seven steps will position your product as the no-brainer solution to the painful problem your audience is struggling with.

Set some time aside to write killer sales copy for all of your "advanced content" products or services (see Chapter 24). You'll need an online description page for each one. So do it. Do it now. Get it done. You'll be excited when you're done and you'll be one big step closer to making money online.

Implementation Checklist

- ☐ Focus on each of your products individually.
- ☐ Take notes for each of the seven steps.
- ☐ Write each section of the sales sequence.
- ☐ Put it all together and work on the flow.
- ☐ Spend extra time on the call to action.
- ☐ Ask friends to read it and provide feedback.
- ☐ Compare notes and ideas with a colleague.

Part Three

Build Your Website and Blog

Chapter 26

Website Development

Can you build a killer website for free?

Yes, you can. These days, there are countless options that allow you to build your own website. And doing it yourself doesn't mean you have to settle for some amateur-looking site either. Let's start with the heavyweights. There are a variety of platforms that are referred to as "open source," meaning they were developed under the GNU (or general public license) and they are entirely free to use. Although open source had its beginnings back in the '60s, the term became more widely used after Netscape released its source code in 1998. Today, open source refers to software developed by and for the public. Anyone can contribute to it and anyone can use it. No charge.

These open source website platforms are often referred to as "Web application frameworks" or "content management systems." They allow you to build impressive websites through a back-end administrative interface (also called a dashboard or control panel). Although these open source platforms all vary slightly, most of their interfaces include buttons like "create a page" or "insert an image" or "add a link," allowing you to build your website from the ground up, one page at a time. There are three primary platforms in this area: Joomla, Drupal, and WordPress. Joomla is the most powerful but also the most complicated. WordPress is less powerful but incorporates blog functionality and is probably (statistics are hard to find) the most commonly used. Drupal is essentially in the middle in terms of functionality and third place in terms of usage volume.

The Tactical Execution website is built on WordPress and I haven't spent a dime on it so far. I did it all myself. Even the graphic images were free. I either created them in Word or found them on public clipart databases. Amateur, I admit, but it works. Within one month of installing WordPress for the

79

first time, my website already had more than 250 pages of content, improving its ranking with the search engines. I was able to quickly add pages and copy content I had created for other purposes beforehand. Is my website a great site? Absolutely not. But it gets the job done: it's doing exactly what I need it to do. And I was able to build it myself. Freedom!

Please note that while building a website can indeed be free, you still have to host it somewhere. Websites have text and graphics and all those files have to be stored in a server somewhere, and that's what website hosting is all about. But don't worry. You can get a good hosting account these days for about $6 per month. I recommend either GoDaddy.com or HostGator.com. Both of them offer one-click installation for the major open source platforms (including all three mentioned above). That means you can literally select the platform you'd like and click a button to have it installed on your hosting account.

I'm obviously a big fan of open source platforms but there are other options as well. For starters, both Microsoft and Google have introduced website–building platforms and are eager to find new users. Microsoft Office Live and Google Sites are both free platforms and are well integrated with their related applications. Most large hosting companies also have website–building platforms available for their customers. Most of them charge a higher monthly hosting fee if your site is built on their platform and I discourage you from using them. There are just too many free alternatives. The trend is clear. Everyone is trying to provide easier ways for average people to build impressive websites. It makes the most sense to align yourself with an open source platform like WordPress and let the technology push you forward.

Implementation Checklist

- ☐ Look into WordPress, Joomla, and Drupal.
- ☐ Research each to see which you like best.
- ☐ Visit the Microsoft Office Live website.
- ☐ Visit the Google Sites website.
- ☐ Visit your hosting company's website.
- ☐ Commit to one platform and get started.
- ☐ Start slow and build one page at a time.
- ☐ Grow and improve your site as you learn.
- ☐ Compare notes and ideas with a colleague.

Chapter 27

The Blogosphere

Do you hate the word "blog"?

If you do, you're not alone. For a lot of people, the word "blog" represents a younger generation they don't understand, technology they find intimidating, and an Internet culture that's passing them by. Whether you love blogs or hate blogs, the facts speak for themselves. Blogs get more traffic than static websites. Blogs are favored by the search engines and all the latest and greatest online tools cater directly to blogs. Bottom line: If you're not blogging, you're missing out on most of today's online opportunities. If you're not that familiar with blogs, they look a lot like websites. In fact, you've probably been on blogs and not even realized it. The difference is in the plumbing. The information is organized differently, but the blog "culture" also represents a significant departure from the old static websites that used to dominate the Internet. We'll be discussing that in future chapters.

Another significant characteristic of a blog is the "subscribe" function. Blogs have something called an RSS feed. It stands for Really Simple Syndication and it's this RSS feed that facilitates the subscription. If you have a blog and I subscribe to it, and if you update your blog with a new post, I don't have to visit your blog to see what you posted. It can get *pushed* to me through the RSS feed (either via e-mail or within a "reader"-like Google Reader). Admittedly, people may or may not subscribe to your blog. That's not the opportunity. The opportunity is that you can integrate different platforms. For example, your Facebook profile can subscribe to your blog. Your LinkedIn profile can subscribe to your blog. Your Twitter profile can subscribe to your blog. What does that mean? It means you can update your blog and click "publish" and have all those other platforms populated automatically! Blogs allow you to leverage your content, your community, and the social media platforms that bind them all together. (We'll be revisiting this topic in Chapter 63.)

In this chapter, it's important to introduce blogs by explaining why they're so heavily favored by the search engines. Search engines look for three primary things when evaluating websites. Blogs cater to all three.

1. The quantity of unique relevant content.
2. The newness or freshness of that content.
3. The link structure surrounding the website.

Blogs are basically online journals and their authors add more content on a regular (sometimes daily) basis. Over time, some blogs accumulate hundreds or even thousands of individual posts, catering directly to the first two things search engines look for.

Next, the culture in the blogosphere is to link out to as many other resources as you possibly can, including other bloggers. Bloggers are fiercely loyal to other bloggers! That means popular blog posts can end up with hundreds of inbound links coming from other blogs. That satisfies the third requirement search engines have. (We'll cover this in Chapter 40.) The net result is that blogs are coming up higher and higher on search engine rankings. That means they're getting more traffic from the search engines and more exposure in general.

Keep in mind that you can easily hire other people to blog on your behalf. New and innovative companies have adopted these strategies to gain online exposure and it's working like a charm. We talked about this in Chapter 17. Put an ad on Craigslist or Google for "ghost writers" and hire some young college students to blog about your field. You could pay them per post and bonus them based on the traffic their posts receive. It's performance-based compensation and adds directly to your website traffic, revenue, and profits.

Implementation Checklist

- ☐ Blogs allow readers to subscribe.
- ☐ Blogs can integrate with other platforms.
- ☐ Blogs are favored by search engines.
- ☐ Blogs get more traffic than static websites.
- ☐ Consider building a blog-based website.
- ☐ Consider hiring others to write content.
- ☐ Compare notes and ideas with a colleague.

Chapter 28

Negative Comments

Are you scared of negative comments?

One of the characteristic features of a blog is that readers can leave comments that remain on the site for future readers to see. In fact, today's social Internet is full of opportunities for perfect strangers to rate your content and post comments. Many people (and businesses) are reluctant to post their content because they're worried about negative comments. This is an area where the younger generation and the older generation have very different perceptions. Older people think this constant ability to comment is a *bad* thing. Younger people think it's a *good* thing. Which is it? The answer depends on how you handle the situation.

Consider a restaurant that receives a negative comment on Yelp about their spaghetti. "The spaghetti sucks." If the restaurant has verified their account on Yelp (see Chapter 48 for more details), they have the ability to respond to each comment. So what should they do? Get mad? Maybe, but there's a better way. Consider the following response:

"Thank you for telling us what nobody else would. We've changed the recipe. Among other things, we're now using ground turkey instead of beef and we're also using organic whole wheat pasta. Please come back and try it again."

Personally, I'd be curious to try the spaghetti. You may feel different, but the point stands. There are productive and unproductive ways to reply to negative comments. The first rule: always reply. Explain how you're fixing the problem. Make sure your response is right beside the comment so that anyone who reads the comment will also read your response. I remember when I got my first negative comment on my "Beyond the Rate" podcast series. That was an educational series about the mortgage business that I recorded in 2006. Anyway, the comment was on the fourth episode. Actually, it was quite vicious. The guy really called me out. He totally disagreed with my thesis and gave a litany of reasons why he was right and I was wrong.

I was mad. Oh boy, was I mad. At first, I started thinking of all the things I wanted to say to that guy—stormrider718, whoever he was. I wanted to tear him down! I strategized all the different things I could do to make his life difficult. But I waited. Thank God. I slept on it. When I woke up the next morning, I realized he was basically right. I hadn't supported my argument. I just spewed out my opinion without any supporting evidence (even though I had plenty). Bottom line: my podcast was practically begging people to post counterarguments.

If you listen to my whole podcast series (it's still available online), you will notice that, starting in the fifth episode, my statements include a lot more supporting evidence. In other words, those later episodes are better than the first four. That guy—stormrider718, the guy I was so angry with at first—ended up helping me improve my podcasts. Negative comments are a blessing in disguise, but you need a lot of self-discipline to see that. You need to hold yourself back at first. Force yourself to wait 24 hours before reacting. It's difficult, I know. But it's so important. If you wait out your initial reaction, you'll soon see the opportunity.

Ironically, negative comments are the best thing you can hope for. They tell you how to improve your business. The faster you find those negative comments, the faster you can improve your business. The truth is that you should almost encourage negative comments! If people absolutely hate you, they're usually pretty quick to say so. But if they have three good things to say and one bad thing to say, they'll usually say the three good things and skip over the bad. How do you uncover that one bad thing? It's way more important to your business than the good things. If you had to improve three things about my product or service, what would they be? Get creative.

What about that *one* guy (or gal) who's seems to be on a mission to destroy your business by posting a negative rant on your blog? What do you do about him or her? Well, you can't do much. But it's okay. If you have 15 four- and five-star reviews and then one absolutely awful review, it sticks out like a sore thumb. Trust that the average person will recognize that as quickly as you do. Once again, I recommend responding to a negative comment as best you can, but there will be some individuals you'll never be able to appease. The important thing to remember is that your response is only 5 percent intended for the person who wrote it; the other 95 percent is intended for all the other people who will read the original comment followed by your response thereafter. I recently stayed at the Fontainebleau Hotel in Miami Beach, Florida. Upon checkout, I got my receipt in an envelope along with a business card suggesting I post comments on TripAdvisor. Brilliant. Don't hide in a cave, fearing negative comments. Instead, get as many comments as you can and trust that they will average out to accurately reflect the quality of service you provide.

Implementation Checklist

- ☐ Don't fear negative comments.
- ☐ See negative comments as opportunities.
- ☐ Expect bad comments from time to time.
- ☐ Trust that the average will reflect reality.
- ☐ Always reply to comments, good or bad.
- ☐ Wait 24 hours before replying to bad comments.
- ☐ Compare notes and ideas with a colleague.

Chapter 29

SEO: Keyword Saturation

Do people find you on Google?

The vast majority of websites get very few visitors through search engines. Why? Because they might appear on page 20 (or worse) of the search results for the keyword phrases being targeted. Most searchers never get past page one or two of the results. Just look at a basic example. As of this writing, a search for the keyword phrase "Internet marketing" brings up more than 165 million results, but Google's first page only has 10 listings. Assuming the searcher looks through two pages of results, 164,999,980 listings never even get seen. Getting ranked high on search engines like Google has become a science. It's referred to as search engine optimization (or SEO for short) and the next four chapters introduce some powerful tricks you can use to optimize your website for the search engines.

Let's start at the beginning. As we mentioned in Chapter 27, search engines like Google look for the following three primary factors when determining website rankings:

1. The quantity of unique relevant content.
2. The newness or freshness of that content.
3. The link structure surrounding the website.

This chapter elaborates on the first factor. Chapter 30 elaborates on the third factor and Chapter 31 introduces a great SEO trick. The second factor speaks for itself. Don't let your website get stale. Continue to add more content and make adjustments to existing content. Keep it fresh. Google loves new content!

Let's jump into that first factor: the quantity of unique relevant content. Clearly, the basic message is that more is better. A 400-page website generally ranks higher than a 4-page website. But even if your site is not monstrously huge in terms of number of pages, there are things you can do within the content to make your site more search engine friendly.

First, Google loves sentences and paragraphs. Avoid bulleted lists and hidden text. Whenever possible, put your content into standard sentences and paragraphs. Keywords, keywords, keywords. We talked about keyword research in Chapters 12 and 13 and here's where they belong! Pick about a dozen primary keyword phrases and use them naturally but consistently in the following places:

1. The primary domain name, if possible.
2. The page title and, ideally, the page URL.
3. Any main subhead (H1) tags throughout your site.
4. The title tag and page description.
5. The alt tags of all images on your site.
6. The first paragraph of your page content.
7. Throughout the rest of your page content.

Let's expand on a few of these. The first point, the primary domain name, is an often-missed opportunity. If you haven't already registered a domain name for your website, try to find one that incorporates your most important keyword. It helps.

The second point, the page title and the page URL, are also overlooked frequently. A lot of websites are structured such that the individual page URLs end in things like ".com/content/pageid?=63956/." Nothing could be less helpful from an SEO perspective. The page URL is valuable real estate. Whenever possible, incorporate your page title into the page URL such as ".com/how-to-rank-high-on-search-engines/". Using your primary keywords in the page title and also in the page URL dramatically improves the odds of having that page rank high for the keywords used.

The third point, the HI tags, is important as well. If you have any headings on your page, always use H1 tags and incorporate keywords into the heading. H1 is an HTML tag that refers to Heading 1. HTML also includes H2, H3, and H4 tags for lower level headings. Google considers H1 tags to be important and gives greater consideration to the words in H1 tags than to the words in normal content. Take advantage of that by using H1 tags on every page and incorporating your keywords in those headings.

Most websites also don't take advantage of opportunities to make themselves more attractive to search engines when it comes to the fourth point listed previously: title tags and page descriptions. These cater directly to search engines but most websites don't even use title tags and page descriptions (see Chapter 14). That's a major missed opportunity. Not only will title tags and page descriptions have an immediate impact on your website's ranking but they also determine the text that shows up on the search engine results page.

The fifth point, alt tags of images on your site, is another opportunity. Every image you put on your website can have an alt tag (also part of the HTML coding language). Alt tags determine the words that show up when people use their cursor to scroll over the top of the image. Google looks at alt tags as an indication of what the image (and hence, the page) is about, so make sure you load your alt tags with keywords.

The sixth point might seem trivial but it makes a difference. Google likes to see the primary keywords in the first paragraph of the page and have them match the keywords being used in the title tag and meta tags. In other words, Google likes consistency between the title, meta tags, first paragraph copy and the rest of the page content. So make sure your keyword Focus is consistent throughout the page.

Once you've made adjustments to your website, you'll have to wait for Google to re-index your site before you'll see the results. That can take anywhere from a few hours to a few weeks depending on how often your site gets indexed. You can resubmit your site map to accelerate the process. The Google Webmaster Tools is the easiest place to do that (we'll introduce that platform in Chapter 32). You can also submit individual URLs manually at the following location:

www.google.com/addurl

If you follow this chapter's suggestions regarding placement of keywords in your website, you should see dramatic improvement in your search engine ranking.

Implementation Checklist

- ☐ Write in full sentences and paragraphs.
- ☐ Register a domain name with keywords.
- ☐ Include keywords in page titles and URLs.
- ☐ Use H1 tags and include your keywords.
- ☐ Always use title tags and page descriptions.
- ☐ Include keywords in all image alt tags.
- ☐ Use keywords in the first paragraph.
- ☐ Use keywords throughout page content.
- ☐ Compare notes and ideas with a colleague.

Chapter 30

SEO: Inbound Links

How many inbound links do you have?

Chapter 27 introduced the three primary factors the search engines look for when ranking websites. Here they are again:

1. The quantity of unique relevant content.
2. The newness or freshness of that content.
3. The link structure surrounding the website.

The third factor is extremely important. Basically, Google considers an inbound link from a related content website to be a vote of confidence in your website. The more votes you have, the better your website is presumed to be. Now, there are a lot of inbound links that don't mean much. Untargeted web directories that do not present related content are a good example. "Link farms" are another. As a result, Google gives you credit for some links but not others.

Google also looks at a second level to see how many links are pointing to the websites that are linking to you. So, if I had an inbound link from a website that had five inbound links itself, it would count for less than a different inbound link coming from a website that had 100 inbound links. This methodology forms the foundation of the Google PageRank score. PageRank is a score Google calculates to reflect the relevance and importance of a website. The range is between 0 and 10, with 10 being the highest score. The Google PageRank score is calculated on an exponential curve so most websites have a score of 3 or lower. A PageRank of 4 is definitely above average. Predictably, Google has a PageRank of 10. Yahoo! has a 9. You can easily check your PageRank by installing the Google Toolbar on your browser or by using one of the many Google PageRank Checkers on the Internet. Just search for "google pagerank checker" on Google to find one. You can also see the inbound links Google gives you credit for by entering the following in Google's search window:

link:www.WebsiteName.com

Back to inbound links. A link from a PR7 (an abbreviation for a website with a PageRank score of 7) is far more valuable than a link from a PR2. In fact, you could probably have 1,000 inbound links from PR2 websites and still rank lower than a competitor that has just one link from a PR7. The number and quality of your inbound links determines your PageRank score. Once you start getting inbound links from PR5+ websites, your Page-Rank score goes up quickly. But for now, let's take a look at some inbound links you can easily create all by yourself. Basically, we're looking for other related content websites to link to your website. There are many places where you can build a free website to use as a "feeder" website to link to your primary "hub" website. Here are a few possibilities:

1. WordPress.com
2. Blogger.com
3. Squidoo.com
4. Weebly.com
5. Webs.com
6. Sites by Google
7. Geocities by Yahoo!
8. Angelfire by Lycos

In each case, you can build a site for yourself without paying a penny. You can then load it with related content and include links to the precision-optimized pages on your primary hub website. You can even optimize the links. Google looks at the anchor text (the words carrying the link) as an indication of what the target website is about. If you anchor the link to the words "Internet marketing services," for example, the target website ranks higher for those words. Building a "feeder" website is an incredibly powerful SEO strategy. Not only are you creating one-way inbound links to your primary website but you can put those links on the exact keywords you're trying to target.

Following this strategy, a lot of successful Internet marketers build their businesses on a "three-blog network." They build their primary hub website and then build two other blogs: one on WordPress.com and the other on Blogger.com, building each to a PageRank 4 or higher. The result is a powerful SEO triangle they can use to quickly build impressive rankings for new precision-optimized blog posts or new pages. Please note: you do *not* need to do this to be successful online. Building three blogs is obviously a lot more work than building just one. A strategy like this is more important for advanced affiliate marketers who make 100 percent of their income online. My objective here is to show you what's possible and how the game is played. If this strategy fits your intentions, allocate some time to build two or three feeder websites using the platforms listed above. Load them all with related content and link them all to your primary website. Also, make sure they all link to each other, creating a virtual net for the search engine spiders.

Obviously, these feeder sites all begin with a PageRank of 0, so the inbound links won't mean much at the beginning. But it's a start and you can continue to build them up as time goes on. Add content and keep them fresh. The point is these are all things you control yourself. You don't have to ask anybody's permission. There are many other strategies for building a robust link structure around your website and we'll discuss many of them in the coming chapters.

Implementation Checklist

- ☐ Identify your primary keyword phrases.
- ☐ Build "feeder" sites on different platforms.
- ☐ Load feeder sites with related content.
- ☐ Add links to your primary "hub" website.
- ☐ Anchor all links on targeted keywords.
- ☐ Ensure all feeder sites link to each other.
- ☐ Keep the content on feeder sites fresh.
- ☐ Compare notes and ideas with a colleague.

Chapter 31

SEO: Surrogate Homepages

How many homepages does your website have?

The conventional wisdom that your website has one homepage is not necessarily true. You can have multiple pages on your website that *act* like homepages. In fact, you can design dozens of pages that look like homepages but are actually buried somewhere on your website and are precision-optimized for a particular keyword phrase. My Tactical Execution website has 68 homepages. One is my *actual* homepage but there are 67 others that target various keyword phrases. I call them "surrogate homepages." Each one looks similar to my actual homepage. Depending on what you search for, Google lists the most appropriate one.

Google has no inherent preference for a website's actual homepage. It looks at all pages equally and delivers the pages best suited to the search query. When someone searches for a particular phrase and Google delivers one of my surrogate homepages among the search results, the searcher doesn't care if it's my actual homepage or not. The important thing is that the searcher finds the information he or she is looking for.

Obviously, my primary homepage is: www.tacticalexecution.com.

The other 67 homepages each target a different geographic location along with the phrase "Internet marketing services." For example, I target San Francisco, Oakland, Berkeley, and a variety of other municipalities in California's Bay Area, each with the same phrase. One such page can be found at the following URL:

www.tacticalexecution.com/contact/san-francisco-internet-marketing-services

As you can see, the page is called "San Francisco Internet marketing services." I have similar pages for "Oakland Internet marketing services," "Berkeley Internet marketing services," and so on. These keyword phrases are also included in the page's URL as well as the title tag, page description, alt tags, and body text. These precision-optimized pages each rank nicely for the phrases they target. Think about it. If someone were to do a search for the phrase "Berkeley Internet marketing services," my website would offer an exact match, at least in terms of the page title and URL. The thing to remember is that Google slices and dices Internet content. It doesn't distinguish between your homepage and all the other pages on your website. If one particular page buried deep in your website is the best match for the keywords being searched for, that's the page that comes up in the Google search results.

The pages described above are precision-optimized for one particular keyword phrase; I have 67 of these pages, each targeting a slightly different phrase. The idea is to provide the search engines with a perfect destination page for someone searching for that particular keyword phrase. I did this for a past client who had a hauling and garbage removal business. I built the site on WordPress and created 27 surrogate homepages, each precision-targeting a different local city. His site is now a PageRank 4 (see Chapter 30 for a definition) and ranks on the first page of Google results for more than 100 relevant keyword phrases. More than half of his business comes from his website.

This use of multiple "homepages" boils down to an understanding of how search engines work. People who find your website through a search engine may or may not land on your actual homepage first. For that reason, you should build your entire site such that each page could act as a homepage if necessary. Build pages that cater to specific keyword phrases. If you know a keyword phrase that's searched for frequently (see Chapter 13), build a page all about that phrase. Build an entire section about it! Give the search engines a reason to direct their users to your website.

Make sure these precision-optimized pages are well integrated into your website with plenty of links leading to them from other content-packed pages on your site. Google looks at the internal link structure of a website almost as much as it looks at the external link structure. Most websites are full of links like "click here" and "read more," but these phrases do nothing to enhance a site's rankings for relevant keywords. They tell Google that the website is about "click here" and "read more" but that's not true. The website isn't about "click here." It's about your business. So put the links on your primary keywords, not on phrases like "click here." Then point those links at your precision-optimized surrogate homepages.

These "internal links" (links coming from within the same website) are still considered endorsements of the target page, and they will improve your site's search engine ranking as a result. Cross-link all the pages on your website with descriptive text links; it's one of the best ways to optimize your search engine ranking.

Implementation Checklist

☐ Identify your top keyword phrases.
☐ Build one page all about each phrase.
☐ Include the phrase in the title and URL.
☐ Treat these pages as if they're homepages.
☐ Welcome visitors who see that page first.
☐ Build content that caters to search engines.
☐ Maximize internal links to targeted pages.
☐ Compare notes and ideas with a colleague.

Chapter 32

SEO: Diagnostic Tools

What SEO strategies have you missed? What mistakes have you made?

Well, you might ask, if you overlooked an opportunity, how would you know? If you missed something, you missed it. How can you possibly know what tactics you forgot about? The good news is there are plenty of diagnostic tools on the Internet that can help you identify problems or missed opportunities on your website. This chapter introduces three of my favorites. None of them cost any money and they each offer tremendous insights to evaluate and improve your website.

Google Webmaster Tools

www.google.com/webmasters/tools

Like so many other services, Google offers the webmaster tools platform free of charge. The platform has an impressive series of tools you can use to diagnose and fine-tune your website. But before you can do anything, you need to verify that it is, in fact, your website. Don't worry. The verification process is easy. Full instructions are provided. Once verified, you can see any errors the Google spiders experienced when crawling your website. You can also see when Google visited your site last and how many pages they crawled and/or indexed.

One important setting you can specify on the webmaster tools platform is your preferred domain format. In case you didn't know, the "www" at the beginning of most domain names is actually optional. You don't need to include the "www." But the fact that it's optional creates a potential problem. Let's assume your website has the "www" in the complete URL. People

95

who link to your website *without* the "www" experience an automatic redirect. In other words, they will get to your website but only because the computer knows to redirect them. Those redirected links work but they're not precise. Because they're not direct, they don't count as an inbound link from a search engine perspective. Unless . . . Google Webmaster Tools allows you to specify your preferred domain format, either with or without the "www." It's under the Settings tab and I recommend you do that immediately. It ensures that links using either format count as legitimate inbound links. The platform also allows you to view a series of diagnostic summaries, index statistics, internal/external links, and your site map. If you enjoy the techie stuff, you can even analyze and generate a robot.txt file to help Google navigate your website.

Google Webmaster Tools is a powerful platform. Take advantage of it.

The SEO-Browser

www.seo-browser.com

SEO Browser is a brilliant tool that shows you what your website looks like to a search engine. If you visit the site, I recommend you click on the "Advanced" tab in the top right-hand corner and then enter your domain name in the search field. The tool shows you exactly what a search engine sees . . . and what it does *not* see. In other words, it shows you the opportunities you're missing. It shows you places where you can enter more descriptive keywords and headings. The nice thing about the SEO Browser is that you can navigate around your site by clicking on the various links and it stays inside the tool and shows you the search engine perspective throughout. Try it. Browse your site.

SEO Browser also tells you how many internal and external links are on each page. The Google webmaster guidelines recommend you limit the outbound links on any particular page to 100. The SEO Browser tells you immediately if you have exceeded that number. In Chapter 29 we talked about Google's preference for sentences and paragraphs. Remember: Google loves lots of content. The SEO Browser calculates the "text to page weight ratio," offering valuable insight to how search engines evaluate the density of written content on your website.

Another important metric is the size of the page in terms of memory and how quickly it loads. You want your web pages to require as little memory as possible, allowing for quicker load times. Unnecessarily large image files are the most common culprit for slow-loading pages. Before you upload images to your website, make sure they're no more than 72 dots per inch (DPI) and optimized for the web. The SEO Browser provides dozens of valuable insights. Check it out.

Website Grader

http://website.grader.com

Website Grader takes a much broader view of your website and attempts to assess its marketing effectiveness compared with other websites on the Internet. This tool looks at things like page optimization, load times, syndication options, domain registration, and social media presence. The tool isn't that great from a strictly SEO perspective but it does a fantastic job of reminding you about all the different angles of an effective website. Run the tool on your website and see what it suggests. I guarantee it will put a few items on your to-do list.

By the way, the Website Grader scores your site on a 100-point scale, telling you how you ranked compared with all the other sites it looks at. I recommend you ignore this score. Most websites are a complete disaster so a good score from this tool does not necessarily mean you have a great website. It just means you did better than some others. Keep in mind that the top 1 percent of websites account for the vast majority of all online transactions. That means you should be shooting for a score of 99 or higher. Don't get too excited about a Website Grader score of 70 or 80; a score that low means you still have work to do!

Implementation Checklist

- ☐ Visit the Google Webmaster Tools website.
- ☐ Create an account and verify your website.
- ☐ Select your preferred domain format.
- ☐ Check for broken links and other errors.
- ☐ Visit the SEO Browser and click "Advanced."
- ☐ Enter your URL and browse your website.
- ☐ Look for opportunities to add keywords.
- ☐ Ensure each page has less than 100 links.
- ☐ Monitor the "text to page weight ratio."
- ☐ Visit the Website Grader and run your site.
- ☐ Review their suggestions for improvement.
- ☐ Compare notes and ideas with a colleague.

Chapter 33

Google Analytics

Who's visiting your website? Any idea?

Precisely answering this question lies at the heart of online success. You can only improve what you measure. But before we get into determining who exactly your visitors are, I want to explain an important fact of life on the Internet. *There are no secrets!* This is a simple but powerful truth. On the Internet, everything can be tracked. If you're curious what people are searching for, you can find out. If you're curious which products are selling the best, you can find out. If you want to know where people are coming from and where they're going, you can find out. The process of measuring all this online activity is called website analytics, and everything on the Internet can be tracked using this process. Turns out, you can access some amazingly powerful tools without spending a penny . . . enter Google Analytics, stage left.

www.google.com/analytics

Let's break it down. Using Google Analytics, you can see:

- How many people are visiting your website.
- The keywords they used to find you on search engines.
- Which website referred them to you.
- What page they saw first.
- How much time they spent on your site.
- How many pages they visited.
- From what page they exited your site.
- The geographic location of your visitors.
- The browser they're using.

And a host of other facts, figures and statistics!

Installing Google Analytics is simple and free. Once you sign up for an account, the platform gives you a small piece of script (computer code) that you need to put into the footer of your website. Once this process is complete, Google starts tracking all the activity on your website. It's impossible to overstate the importance of this capability. You could track everything you do online and know with certainty what's working and what's not. There are no secrets. You can know without any shadow of a doubt. That's powerful stuff. In the past, you would've had to do surveys or focus groups to gain insights to these topics. No longer. On the Internet, you can see it all.

Let's take one example. Using Google Analytics, you can see your "bounce rate." That's the percentage of people who quickly leave your website after viewing any particular page. Now, just to be clear, you do *not* want people leaving your website. You want them to keep browsing. If they're leaving your site from one particular page, you need to improve that page to keep your visitors interested. With Google Analytics, you could list all of your web pages sorted by their respective bounce rates. The ones with the highest bounce rate are the ones that need the most attention. Work on those pages to keep visitors interested and engaged. Every time you do this one simple exercise, your website will be a bit more effective than it was before. This is just one example, but there are dozens. Google Analytics is a great platform and it gives you the opportunity to systematically improve your website. There are a lot of other platforms that provide analytics data and some of them are very good. You're welcome to use whichever you like. I focused on Google Analytics in this chapter because it's free, powerful, and extremely well used.

Implementation Checklist

- ☐ Sign up for a Google Analytics account.
- ☐ Add the script into the footer of your site.
- ☐ Let the platform start accumulating data.
- ☐ Visit your analytics account regularly.
- ☐ Click on every option; explore everything.
- ☐ See which websites are referring visitors.
- ☐ Check the keywords that bring you traffic.
- ☐ Notice how long people stay on your site.
- ☐ Check which pages they go to the most.
- ☐ Never stop looking for more insights.
- ☐ Compare notes and ideas with a colleague.

Chapter 34

Understand Analytics Data

"My website gets 30,000 visitors per month!"

That's what a very talkative guy once told me at a networking event. He wasn't the first person to proudly share such information with me. People are often quick to blurt out how much traffic their websites are supposedly getting. Turns out, you can find out a lot about someone else's website all on your own. But before we get to that, let me explain a few important distinctions.

First, a "hit" is not a "visitor." A hit is any click on any link on your website. If you have a bunch of links and someone visits your site and starts browsing around, they can easily rack up 20 or 30 hits during one visit. Most people who claim their website is getting thousands of visitors are misreading their analytics. Those websites might be getting thousands of hits but far fewer visitors. In the case of the guy above who claimed 30,000 visitors, I later found out his website was only getting about 1,500 visitors per month—not bad, but not great either. Going a step further, a visitor is not the same as an "absolute unique visitor." If you visit your own website twice each day, you could be accounting for 50 or 60 visits (and 1,000+ hits) each month. When reading your analytics, you want to see how many *absolute unique visitors* you're getting. That's the important number.

Here in the United States, you can get a fairly good idea how many visitors a site is getting by checking its Alexa ranking. Alexa is the largest third party traffic monitoring site on the Internet. With a few million people using their browser toolbar, Alexa can estimate the traffic to different websites based on the browsing activity of their users.

www.alexa.com

In Europe and Asia, Alexa does not have as many users so the traffic statistics are less reliable. But here in America, you can get a good idea how popular a given site is by checking on Alexa. What does that mean? It means that you now have a tool at your disposal every time someone tries to impress you with their traffic statistics. And why would that matter? Simple. Everyone's looking for affiliates, sponsors, advertisers, and partners, and it's good to know which ones have real traffic and which ones are just blowing smoke.

The guy I told you about at the beginning of this chapter wanted me to give him exclusive rights to sell my educational CDs. When he first proposed the idea, I considered it. But then I got back to my office and checked him out on Alexa—what a fraud. My site was getting more traffic than his! By the way, a higher score on Alexa is not what you want. It's the lower scores that are good. For example, the number one website is the one with the most traffic. As of this writing, Google is number one, Facebook is number two, and YouTube is number three. Any website with an Alexa rank of 400,000 or lower is probably getting at least 100 visitors per day. Sites with a rank of 1,000,000 or higher are getting less than 50 visitors per day, and a website with an Alexa rank higher than 2,000,000 is getting almost no traffic at all.

Here are a couple other tricks you should be aware of. When you go to Google, you can enter some codes to learn things about any given website.

site:www.WebsiteName.com

This displays all the individual pages on the website, allowing you to see exactly how big the website is.

link:www.WebsiteName.com

This displays all the online locations linking to the website, allowing you to see the total number of inbound links as well as where those links are coming from.

As mentioned in Chapter 30, you can also learn the Google PageRank of any particular website. The Google toolbar provides this information or you could just type "google pagerank checker" into Google to find tons of places where you can enter a URL and determine its Google PageRank. Keep in mind that the PageRank score ranges from 0 to 10 where 10 is the best. It's calculated on an exponential curve so a PageRank of 4 or higher is actually pretty good and the jump from 4 to 5 is big. Scores higher than 5 are increasingly significant as you move up the ladder. The point is that if a particular website has a Google PageRank of 2 or 3, it's probably not getting a lot of organic traffic from search engines. Once the site has a PageRank of 4 or higher, it's probably coming up fairly high on Google searches and getting some respectable traffic as a result.

These four things—the Alexa ranking, the number of pages on the site, the number of inbound links, and the Google PageRank score—will give you a pretty good idea of the significance of any website, including your own. These are all little tricks you can use to become a savvier Internet user. Use them to evaluate your own progress and cut through all the hot air on today's Internet!

Implementation Checklist

- ☐ Check your Alexa traffic ranking.
- ☐ Check your number of pages on Google.
- ☐ Check your inbound links on Google.
- ☐ Check your Google PageRank score.
- ☐ Monitor your progress over time.
- ☐ Check the statistics for your competitors.
- ☐ Verify claims made by big talkers.
- ☐ Compare notes and ideas with a colleague.

Chapter 35

Making Sales Online

Are you selling your product or service online?

In the last section, we discussed your expertise and how to categorize that information into beginner, intermediate, and advanced content. Chapter 25 introduced the Motivating sales sequence to help you write effective sales copy for your advanced content products and services. Regardless of what your advanced content is, you need to have a way to sell it online. You need a way to process the actual transactions. This chapter will look at a few of the many websites that facilitate online sales by providing product hosting and shopping cart services. These options make it incredibly easy to start making sales on the Internet.

Perhaps the best known online platform for making sales online is eBay. Most people know eBay as an auction site where you can make your products available for open bidding, but that's only the beginning of what the site offers.

www.ebay.com

eBay allows its users to create their very own eBay store, featuring all of their products in one place. You can then put certain popular products into the public auction and use them to entice shoppers into your store. Also, eBay owns the widely used PayPal platform, making it easy to send and receive money securely. It's worthwhile noting that eBay is one of the highest traffic websites on the Internet. It's crawling with literally millions of shoppers all the time. I call that a "raging river" and it's a great place to put your product in front of a massive buying audience quickly. There are endless resources devoted to leveraging the eBay opportunity and I recommend you simply search for "selling products on eBay" on Google to get started.

eBay isn't the only place where you can create your own store. Yahoo! offers a similar opportunity. The Yahoo! Shopping Network is a powerful and flexible platform that gives anyone an easy way to sell products on the Internet.

http://shopping.Yahoo.com

Of course, one of the largest online retailers is Amazon. Well, as luck would have it, you can sell your products there too! Amazon has a number of seller programs, including the Advantage program, making it easy to upload products and sell them to the public.

http://advantage.amazon.com

Within the Advantage program, Amazon fulfils the orders for you. That means they ship your product to the customer. They also have a second seller platform where you fulfill the orders yourself. With eBay and Yahoo!, the product delivery is always left to you. With eBay and Yahoo!, you're the retailer. With Amazon Advantage, on the other hand, you're the wholesaler and Amazon is the retailer. Because of that, the Advantage program takes a much larger cut. They get the first 55 percent of your product's sales price. But then, whenever you see a reduced price on Amazon, that discount comes out of *their* share, not yours.

Keep in mind that these programs are changing all the time. New websites are popping up every day and that increased competition improves these arrangements for sellers over time. Check to see what the latest programs offer and use the platforms that best suit your situation.

There are dozens of other places where you can sell your products, particularly if the product is digital (like an e-book or an audio file). Zipidee is a great example. On Zipidee, you can upload your digital products and sell them to the public.

www.zipidee.com

The biggest advantage of these platforms is that they all have massive traffic already. That means you can put your product in front of their buyers, and not worry quite as much about generating your own traffic. Driving traffic is usually the hardest part! Of course, you can also drive traffic to your own website or blog and then link through to these platforms. That means you can include a link on your sales page (with the killer sales copy you wrote in Chapter 25) that points to the website where your visitors can actually purchase the product.

Implementation Checklist

- [ ] Visit eBay and read about their programs.
- [ ] Explore the Yahoo! Shopping Network.
- [ ] Research the latest programs on Amazon.
- [ ] Check out Zipidee and look for others.
- [ ] Evaluate based on credibility and profits.
- [ ] Sell your products on the winning websites.
- [ ] Link to your products from your own site.
- [ ] Compare notes and ideas with a colleague.

Chapter 36

Website Shopping Cart

Do you want your very own shopping cart?

Chapter 35 looked at a variety of websites where you can sell your products online, but we didn't look at selling products directly on your own website. That's what this chapter is about. Having your own shopping cart is a lot easier than it used to be. There was a time when you had to build all the code into your own website. You had to integrate your website with a merchant account to accept VISA or MasterCard, and you had to integrate that merchant account with your bank account.

It was complicated. No longer.

Today, there are companies that offer out-of-the-box shopping cart solutions that you can easily link to or integrate directly into your own website. In most cases, the people visiting your website don't even realize the shopping cart is being hosted elsewhere.

A great example is 1ShoppingCart.com.

The websites we discussed in the last chapter—eBay, Yahoo!, Amazon, and Zipidee—the ones that host your products and let you sell them using their shopping cart—make money on the product being sold. In other words, they get a cut of your sales price.

With 1ShoppingCart, you can sell whatever you want and get 100 percent of the money. They do, however, charge a fee for the shopping cart itself. 1ShoppingCart also operates as the merchant account so they make some money on the credit card transactions too. But other than that, all the money is yours. There are advantages to both online selling formats and we discussed some of the advantages of the first group in the previous chapter. Here, we'll focus exclusively on 1ShoppingCart and the service they offer.

Please note that there are lots of different shopping cart solutions available on the Internet. PayPal offers that functionality, as does Google Checkout, and there are many others. I'm focusing on 1ShoppingCart because their service combines the shopping cart functionality with an e-mail autoresponder. We'll get to that in a second. With 1ShoppingCart, you can sell anything for any price. It can be a $25 e-book, an $800 consulting solution, a $4,000 retreat package, or a $17,000 custom motorcycle. It can also be a subscription or membership package, meaning your customers are automatically charged every month or every year or whatever you specify.

No matter what you're selling, 1ShoppingCart allows you to process online transactions in a flexible and seamless way. Even if you consummate an offline transaction without a computer nearby, you can take a credit card number and process the payment when you get back to the office. 1ShoppingCart has a variety of packages, each offering different levels of functionality. The most inexpensive packages start around $35 per month and their premium option is about $100, plus standard credit card processing fees. The premium option includes an e-mail autoresponder as well. The advantage is that everything exists on the same platform. At the time of this writing, I have my products on a variety of different platforms and my autoresponder with aWeber.

Although I'm very happy with aWeber (and I got grandfathered in so I pay only $19.95 per month), it can be frustrating to maintain content on so many different platforms. Also, if I make a sale on Amazon, I have no way of contacting the customer afterward. They don't give me their e-mail address. With 1ShoppingCart, I would have full contact information for all of my customers. I've considered moving everything over to 1ShoppingCart, just to have it all together.

You might want to think about this too. If you have everything on a single platform such as 1Shopping Cart, you could send different e-mails to different people depending on their individual history with you. If customers purchased one particular product, you could tailor an e-mail acknowledging that. If they subscribed to your intermediate content (Chapter 23) but have not purchased anything yet, you could tailor an e-mail to that as well. And for your best customers—the ones who have bought from you multiple times—you could send special offers that nobody else receives.

It's been proven time and again that marketing is more effective if it's more personalized. The less "canned" your message sounds, the better. You want each reader to feel like you're speaking directly to him or her. 1ShoppingCart can help you accomplish these marketing objectives; it offers a powerful and flexible solution. The platform can calculate sales taxes and shipping rates automatically. It supports affiliate links and up-sell or cross-sell options. It offers secure sockets layer (SSL) encryption for the checkout process (adding security) and makes payment tracking simple. It's not the only solution but it's definitely one of the best.

If you're serious about selling your products and services online, you'll need a shopping cart eventually. You can easily leverage other platforms but having your own comes with some distinct advantages. 1ShoppingCart is one option you should consider.

Implementation Checklist

- ☐ Visit the 1ShoppingCart.com website.
- ☐ Read about their various service options.
- ☐ Research other e-commerce platforms.
- ☐ Think about what you'd like to sell online.
- ☐ Make note of the features you could use.
- ☐ Consider subscribing to their service.
- ☐ Learn how to use the platform thoroughly.
- ☐ Leverage the service wherever possible.
- ☐ Compare notes and ideas with a colleague.

Chapter 37

Outsource Basic Tasks

What tasks can you outsource?

Outsourcing refers to the process of subcontracting work to a third party. In his *New York Times, Wall Street Journal,* and *BusinessWeek* bestseller, *The 4-Hour Workweek,* Tim Ferriss argues that you can outsource a huge portion of the clutter currently monopolizing your daily calendar. Even better, the process can remove a common bottleneck (yourself) and allow your business to thrive in your absence.

Today's online communication tools make it easier than ever to get help from the other side of the world. And guess what? The cost of living is very different in some of those places than it is here in America. What does that mean? It means that getting help won't cost you nearly as much as it would if you hired locally. A lot of people get frustrated at the process of outsourcing job functions to other parts of the world. They argue it contributes to the local unemployment rate and sabotages our domestic economy. And in many ways, they're right. It does. But the trends are clear and your competition will take advantage of the opportunities even if you don't. These realities are often difficult to swallow, but they're also impossible to ignore. There are highly skilled people in other parts of the world who are happy to help you for four or five dollars per hour. How can you use those resources to build your business?

I've done it myself. I have a virtual assistant in Chennai, India, and her name is Uma. I started working with her in 2009 and have really come to appreciate her contributions. First, there is an 11-hour time difference so she is awake while I'm sleeping and vice versa. When I have a project for her to work on, I e-mail detailed instructions in the evening before I go to bed. Eight hours later, I wake up and boot up my computer . . . and the work is done! Does this arrangement always work perfectly smoothly? No. Are there misunderstandings? Yes. Are there mistakes? Of course. Is it frustrating to type out detailed step-by-step instructions for tasks I could easily do myself? Absolutely. But there is also a learning curve in place. Uma is on this learning curve and so am I. Over time, our working relationship gets better and better.

Uma has helped me build databases of conferences around the world. She has helped me submit proposals to those conferences. She has helped me build and manage my Twitter following. She has helped me reach out to book reviewers on Amazon. She has helped me contact bloggers who might be interested in this book. All of these are basic but time-consuming tasks. And in many cases, they are tasks I would never have found time for had I not had her help. Don't think about what you are *currently* doing. Think about what you *could* be doing. Think about the simple tasks that you don't have time for but that would help build your business.

The following two online platforms make this process easy:

www.elance.com

www.odesk.com

On either of these sites, you can post your job and receive dozens of proposals within days. Take a couple hours and make a list of the tasks you'd like to get done. Write down all the skills that would be required, such as good written English or proficiency with Excel or familiarity with a particular website. Then compile those skills into a job description and post it on Elance or oDesk. You'll be amazed at the responses you get.

I highly recommend Tim Ferriss's book. He takes the concept of outsourcing to a whole new level. The book is packed with content and he has demonstrated the power of his approach by living an extraordinary life himself. Tim is a very smart guy and he's written an excellent book. Buy a copy. Of course, *this* book (yeah, the one you're reading) is the perfect place to start. It's full of tactical strategies you can use to promote your business, but it all takes time. The chapters each add a few more items to your to-do list. Why not find a virtual assistant and train him or her to help you complete the tasks?

It's a new world out there. Think bigger. Think globally. Take advantage of everything you can, including the skilled labor in Argentina, India, or the Philippines. Your virtual assistant can be your secret weapon. And believe me, once your friends catch wind of what you're doing, they'll all be jealous. Give it a try. Pick one project, say 40 hours worth of work. Post it on Elance or oDesk and hire someone at $5 per hour to get it done. It'll only cost you $200 and the process will give you firsthand knowledge of the potential. You never know. You might get addicted! I know I did.

Implementation Checklist

- [ ] Make a list of tasks you could outsource.
- [ ] Pick the easiest one to start.
- [ ] Identify the skills required to get it done.
- [ ] Compile the skills into a job description.
- [ ] Post the job on Elance and oDesk.
- [ ] Allocate $200 USD for a 40-hour task.
- [ ] Write detailed instructions for the task.
- [ ] Select a provider to complete the task.
- [ ] Give them the instructions and try it.
- [ ] Evaluate the results of the project.
- [ ] If it was a success, outsource more tasks.
- [ ] If there were problems, don't give up.
- [ ] Calibrate the process and try it again.
- [ ] Compare notes and ideas with a colleague.

Part Four

Populate Internet Properties

Chapter 38

Internet Directories

Are Internet directories useless?

There was a time when you could accumulate valuable one-way inbound links by registering your website on many online directories. Those days are gone. The search engines no longer give much credence to directory links. Are there exceptions? Absolutely. The Open Directory Project (also known as DMOZ from directory.mozilla.org), for example, still offers a valuable link—and there are others. These directories are still worth registering with, but they're not the reason for this chapter.

There are more and more directories that list companies operating within one industry or another. Dentists, chiropractors, hauling companies, real estate agents, insurance brokers, contractors, and salons all come to mind. A single industry is often referred to as a "vertical." Getting listed on directories within your vertical can be very valuable, primarily because prospective customers are finding these directories and using them the way people once used the Yellow Pages. In many cases, getting registered within these directories doesn't cost anything because the websites hosting them want to cultivate a complete list, making their directory more valuable and attracting more visitors as a result.

Go to Google and search for your keywords along with the word "directory." Browse through the first five or ten pages and see what you can find. Within an hour, you'll probably find two or three directories—maybe more. Get your company listed along with a link to your website. Various directories will be set up slightly differently but look for links like "get registered," "create an account," "submit a link," or "add your listing" to submit your information. A few years ago, people registered with online directories to get inbound links. Today, the search engine algorithms have diminished that opportunity. But the more specific directories still offer value—not for search engines but for humans. Getting listed within niche directories can bring you customers.

Your local Chamber of Commerce is another example of a niche directory. Of course, membership in a Chamber of Commerce isn't free but their directories are specific to your location, making them more relevant to users. Other community organizations like Rotary, Kiwanis, and Lions have similar directories for their members. Check with the associations operating in your industry or clubs that cater to your profession. They all offer directories where your listing can attract qualified prospects. Allocate a few hours to search for these directories and register with as many as you can. Make note of the ones that aren't free and prioritize your list for future consideration. Maybe you can afford to get listed with a few right away. Maybe not. Either way, these directories can play a major role in helping you establish your online identity.

Implementation Checklist

- [ ] Google your keywords plus "directory."
- [ ] Try to find directories within your vertical.
- [ ] Register your company on the free directories.
- [ ] Make note of those that aren't free.
- [ ] Register with paid directories when your budget allows.
- [ ] Contact your local Chamber of Commerce.
- [ ] Find local Rotary, Kiwanis, and Lions clubs.
- [ ] Determine the fee and member base.
- [ ] Check the prominence of their websites.
- [ ] Join if it would add to your online presence.
- [ ] Check for associations in your industry.
- [ ] Check for clubs serving your profession.
- [ ] Compare notes and ideas with a colleague.

Chapter 39

Blog Directories

Does anyone know you exist?

If you're like most bloggers, the answer is *no*. A lot of talented "content creators" publish inspiring blog posts that nobody ever reads! Sad but true. The next few chapters discuss blogging best practices and how you can share your brilliance with a global audience. It all begins with awareness. If nobody knows you exist, they have no way of endorsing your content and sharing it with their friends.

Today's Internet offers ever-expanding social media platforms where you can share your content with the world. But before we talk about those platforms in detail, we need to address the basics. There are hundreds of free blog directories on the Internet. You need to get registered on as many of those as you can. Blog directories are similar to the niche directories we discussed in the previous chapter. You won't get a lot of SEO benefits from the directory links. The main benefit is simply to populate the world of bloggers with your existence. Will the directories drive hundreds of unique visitors to your site? No, they won't. But they announce to the Internet world that you are there. Bottom line: You want to be listed in any place where somebody might find you.

In preparation for the project, you need to put some thought into your blog title and description. Even for those who have already finalized these details, it's worth taking a minute to rethink them. The description, in particular, is extremely valuable real estate and you want it to pull readers in by making them curious. Every blog directory requests your blog title and your blog description. Make sure you have these two pieces of information prepared before you get started.

Not surprisingly, there are a few blog directories that are more impor-tant than others. The top sites you should check out first include Technorati .com, BlogCatalog.com, and MyBlogLog.com.

Technorati is much more than just a blog directory; it's a major player in the blogosphere and you should begin your journey by getting listed there. BlogCatalog and MyBlogLog are both online communities where you can accumulate friends and connect with other bloggers. And to give you an idea how big these communities are, there are successful bloggers whose only marketing efforts take place within these platforms.

There are many services that will register your blog with all the major directories for a fee. These fees range from $2 to $200. To find these services, search for "blog directory submission" on Google.

Building a blog is like building a house. You have to start with the foundation. Most bloggers start their blog by installing double-pane windows and decorative planters. Don't make the mistake of focusing first on the cosmetic frills. Start with the foundation. Get your blog listed on all the major directories. After that, there's a long list of things you can do. We'll talk about some items for your to-do list in the coming chapters.

Implementation Checklist

- ☐ Optimize your blog title and description.
- ☐ Register your blog at Technorati.com.
- ☐ Register your blog at BlogCatalog.com.
- ☐ Register your blog at MyBlogLog.com.
- ☐ Search for submission services on Google.
- ☐ Consider using a service to get listed.
- ☐ Announce to the Internet that you exist!
- ☐ Compare notes and ideas with a colleague.

Chapter 40

Outbound Links = Currency

What's the fastest way to make friends on the blogosphere?

Link to other bloggers. Outbound links are the currency of the blogosphere. This may be the most important reality behind effective blogging. Without outbound links, your blog's popularity will grow far slower then it could otherwise. You have to understand that all bloggers are looking for the same things you're looking for. They're looking for traffic. They're looking for an audience. They're looking for exposure.

The second thing you need to understand is that modern marketing is built on an abundance mentality, not a scarcity mentality. The days of keeping your ideas secret and working only to benefit yourself are over. That type of blatant self-interest does far more to harm your business than grow it. Help others. Endorse others. Provide value to your audience. Whenever you find something valuable (even if it's on a competitor's website), link to it and tell your audience about it. Become a beacon of value for your followers. You want your blog to be a single gateway to the *entire universe* of resources in your field. You want the world to know that they can visit your blog and immediately have access to every possible resource they might need to help them achieve their objective. Value leads to trust. Trust leads to sales. People need to trust you first and only then will they buy your product or service. By providing value, you're building trust. And how can you build value on your blog? There are two ways.

First, you can build value by delivering outstanding content yourself. You can write good stuff. Second, you can endorse other people's content by linking to it. If you find something useful on someone else's blog or website, blog about it and include a link. Now, let's look at this from the other side. Do you think the bloggers you link to will appreciate your endorsement? By providing a link, you're willing to divert some of your traffic to their website. Do you think they'll appreciate it? Of course they will. That's exactly what they're looking for. You're helping them out.

It's easy to see who's linking to your blog. You can find out on Google or Technorati but inbound links are also listed on most administrative dashboards too. Certainly, WordPress shows you who's linking to you right on the dashboard.

So, when these bloggers see that you linked to them, what do you think they'll do? If it were me, I would check out your blog and see what you wrote about me. Right? I'd be curious. Wouldn't you? Absolutely. That means the majority of bloggers you link to will visit your blog and see what you're up to. And if they like what you're doing, they might just link back.

That's precisely my point.

By linking to other bloggers, you increase the odds they'll link back to you. At the very least, they'll know you exist. And while you may not control who links to your blog, you certainly control who you link to. In fact, you can link to the most popular blogs in your field! We'll be talking about that in the next chapter.

Blogging is a human activity. By endorsing someone else, you accumulate brownie points. You get in the good graces of your peers. That's where you want to be. Give love, get love. You should link out to as many blogs and websites as you possibly can. It helps you become completely interwoven in the blogosphere. Imagine receiving an e-mail from a fellow blogger who wrote a post all about you and your blog. How would that feel? It would make you happy, wouldn't it? You can *be* that fellow blogger. You can make someone feel like that. You have the power. Use it.

Implementation Checklist

- [ ] Abandon the scarcity mentality.
- [ ] Adopt the abundance mentality.
- [ ] Push value out to your audience.
- [ ] Link to every resource you possibly can.
- [ ] Send e-mails to those you link to.
- [ ] Avoid criticizing. Give love to get love.
- [ ] Compare notes and ideas with a colleague.

Chapter 41

Subscribe to Top Bloggers

Who are the top bloggers in your field?

In Chapter 40, we talked about linking to other bloggers as a way of making friends, gaining exposure and building your link structure. Some people hate that idea because they see it as a direct endorsement of their biggest competitors. If you feel that way, consider changing your mind.

The abundance mentality will rule in the future. It's already dominating the online world today. Share the love, and the links. The very first thing you should do as a blogger is identify the top players in your field. Who's the very best? Who do you respect? Who has the biggest audience? Once you've identified these top bloggers, you should spare no effort in trying to publicly endorse their work. Your willingness to reference these industry leaders directly and link to their resources immediately increases your own stature. You look like a peer rather than an adoring fan. It makes you look like a leader yourself. I highly recommend identifying and subscribing to the top bloggers in your field. Technorati is a great place to find them. So is Google BlogSearch. For me, this category includes people such as Seth Godin, Tim Ferriss, John Reese, Frank Kern, Pete Cashmore, Brendon Burchard, Jeff Walker, Chris Brogan, Gary Vaynerchuk, Peter Shankman, Dan Schawbel, Bob Bly, and Dan Kennedy, among others. Find the leaders in your field and subscribe to their feeds.

By the way, the easiest way to subscribe to these bloggers is to use a "reader" like Google Reader. Most readers are free and provide a great way to follow the latest posts all in one place. When you log on, they provide a list of all the posts published by those you're following, just like a newspaper. You can then scroll through and see what everybody's blogging about. It's also worth mentioning that most of these readers let you search for feeds using keywords or a person's name and then sort the results by the number of subscribers. Although the Internet is full of hidden treasures, it's a pretty safe bet that the gurus in your field already have large followings, making them easy to find.

Once you've identified your industry leaders and subscribed to their feeds using a reader, I recommend checking the latest posts every time you write a post yourself. Get in the habit. By doing so, your awareness skyrockets and you will almost always have other blogs you can link to in your post. This is such a simple strategy, but you'd be amazed how few people take advantage of it. I'm guilty of it myself. Sometimes, I just don't feel like I have the time but I'm always sorry when I skip this step.

I describe the people I follow as "thought leaders." They're usually on the cutting edge of my field: modern entrepreneurship and online marketing. They know what's hot in the market. And reading their posts allows me to stay up-to-date on the latest strategies and add my own contribution to the discussion. If your posts address the hottest topics in your field, you'll be perfectly positioned to capture some of the browsers searching for those keywords on search engines. And if your posts link out to other leaders in your field, your audience will start to grow. Finally, if some of those "thought leaders" start linking back to you, your exposure (and PageRank) could explode quickly. Surround yourself with leaders. Surround yourself with top-quality content. It improves all aspects of your game and your audience benefits as well.

Implementation Checklist

- [ ] Select keywords to describe your field.
- [ ] Visit Technorati and find the top bloggers.
- [ ] Use Google BlogSearch to find other bloggers.
- [ ] Subscribe to the top bloggers in your field.
- [ ] Select a "reader" like Google Reader.
- [ ] Add all your feeds to your reader.
- [ ] Always check your reader before writing.
- [ ] Follow the "hot" topics and discussion.
- [ ] Link to others writing about the same topic.
- [ ] Compare notes and ideas with a colleague.

Chapter 42

Interviews and Guest Bloggers

Do you struggle to find topics to blog about?

For most, the answer is *yes*. When charged with the task of writing two or three blog posts each week, most people freeze. What should I write about? Turns out, there's an easy way to get great content for your blog and you don't have to write anything at all. Doesn't that sound like a get-rich-quick scheme? Well, this one's pretty close. Check it out.

There are, of course, countless "experts" and "gurus" in any industry, including yours. Here's another reality: most of them aren't nearly as successful as they make themselves out to be. Sorry, but it's true. That means all those "industry leaders" are desperately looking for ways to gain additional exposure for themselves. If you contacted some of those experts and asked them if they'd be interested in writing a guest post on your blog, the majority of them would jump at the offer and be grateful for the opportunity. I know. I've done it myself. Here's how it works:

"Hello, [expert's name]. A few months ago, I subscribed to your blog and really enjoy your posts. I'd like to introduce my readers to your work and am curious if you would be interested in writing a guest post on my blog. Please let me know if you can fit it into your schedule."

I've also had people approach me, and I'm always flattered as a result. I haven't agreed to every request but have contributed more than half the time. Now, just to be clear, I suggest you do this with people who you *are* subscribed to and who you *do* follow, at least for a month or two. (See Chapter 41 for more information.) I'm *not* suggesting you spam out to people who you are not familiar with. When you approach people whose work you have some knowledge of, most will be genuinely appreciative of your offer and quick to contribute. Tell them they're welcome to include a link back to their own blog along with a photo and professional bio.

Here's the problem: Most people don't want to do this because they feel like it's effectively an endorsement of their competition. Don't get trapped in this mind-set. By associating with leaders in your field, you're making yourself more valuable to your audience and raising your own profile in the process.

There's a variation on the guest blogger scenario that can draw an even more direct link between you and the experts you approach. Do an interview! You can either do it via e-mail or record it over the phone. If you record a phone conversation, you'll be left with an audio podcast as well as a blog post (once it's transcribed). (See Chapter 51 for more information on podcasting.)

Interviews are generally easier than blog posts for the people you're approaching. The only thing they're committing to is a phone conversation. E-mail them the questions ahead of time so they can formulate their answers. Let them know you'll be recording the call and then schedule a time. There are many ways to record a call, but there are a couple I recommend. First, you can use Skype. It's easy and you can call your expert on his or her regular phone number. If you don't already have a Skype account, sign up for one. It's free. Second, you can use a service such as FreeConferenceCall and ask the expert to call in to your conference call number. As the moderator, you can click "record" and have an audio file ready for download when you're done with the interview.

www.freeconferencecall.com

Valuable content is closer than you might think. There's no secret to finding it. It's no elusive target. Instead, its right in front of you and the thought leaders in your industry are eager to share their ideas with new audiences. There are people who have become recognized experts in their field, *only* by interviewing other experts! It's also worth mentioning that this strategy invites industry leaders into your personal network. You're doing them a favor and they'll appreciate it, even if you're benefiting at the same time. Building relationships with the industry experts in your field is just plain smart! Do interviews. It's truly a win-win.

Implementation Checklist

- ☐ Make a list of industry experts in your field.
- ☐ Become familiar with their expertise.
- ☐ Make a list of questions for each expert.
- ☐ Choose the type of interview: text or audio.
- ☐ If audio, select the method of recording.
- ☐ Contact the experts to propose an interview.
- ☐ Invite them to include a link and photo.
- ☐ Schedule a time and conduct the interview.
- ☐ Send a thank-you card after the interview.
- ☐ Compare notes and ideas with a colleague.

Chapter 43

Blog Carnivals

Would you like your work to be featured in a magazine?

Anyone looking to build exposure for themselves or their business would jump at the opportunity. Not only would it demonstrate your expertise in front of a whole new audience, but it would also give you tremendous credibility in front of your existing followers.

What's a blog carnival?

A blog carnival is like a magazine except that it's online. Certain bloggers host carnivals about one topic or another and anyone can submit blog posts to be considered for inclusion. If the hosting blogger agrees to feature your post, the carnival will introduce your contribution and include a link for interested readers to read your post . . . on your blog. There's a great place to see all the carnivals taking place and submit your posts to those whose topic relates to your content.

http://BlogCarnival.com

This platform allows those hosting carnivals and those contributing to carnivals to connect with each other. All the upcoming carnivals are listed and categorized, making them easy to identify. Once you find a carnival you're interested in, you can submit your work directly to the host.

I used to do this once every couple of weeks. In less than an hour, I could scan the upcoming carnivals and submit my new posts to 10 or 20 carnivals. Obviously, your acceptance rate depends on the quality of your work, but I generally got accepted by at least half the carnivals I submitted to. That means I received up to 10 new one-way inbound links to my blog every two weeks. Not only did that fuel my Google ranking but it also added to my Technorati authority—not to mention all the traffic that found my blog from carnivals hosted elsewhere on the Internet.

As you probably guessed, the second major opportunity lies with hosting a carnival yourself. On BlogCarnival.com, it's very easy to set up your own carnival and let other bloggers start submitting posts to you. You can select those you like and include them in your own carnival. In short order, you'll become a "known quantity" among the most active bloggers in your field.

BlogCarnival.com goes a step further, offering their InstaCarnival feature that provides basic HTML code to cut and paste into your blog. That means it would take you no more than five minutes to publish each edition of your carnival. It couldn't be any easier. Take advantage of this opportunity to expand your online presence.

Blog carnivals represent an active ongoing conversation in the blogosphere—a conversation you can participate in. Your contributions are all that's required to get known in your field. You can quickly establish your reputation as an active contributor in your area of expertise and that can leave you with enhanced credibility within your peer group.

This is the last chapter about effective blogging. We started by discussing the importance of outbound links and how they can encourage others to link back to you. We talked about top bloggers and how you can benefit by subscribing to their blogs. And in this chapter, we introduced blog carnivals and how they can help you become tightly integrated into the blogosphere. These are all fantastic ways to position yourself online. Done consistently, these processes can change your business (and your life) forever.

Implementation Checklist

- [ ] Visit BlogCarnival.com.
- [ ] Search the upcoming carnival listings.
- [ ] Find appropriate carnivals for your posts.
- [ ] Create an account for yourself.
- [ ] Submit recent posts with a description.
- [ ] Consider hosting your own blog carnival.
- [ ] Once logged in, click "Organize new carnival."
- [ ] Schedule a new edition for your carnival.
- [ ] Watch the submissions come in. It's fun!
- [ ] Compare notes and ideas with a colleague.

Chapter 44

Conversations Are Markets

How can you access a *market* on today's social Internet?

I get asked this question all the time. And whether you realize it or not, we've been talking about this subject throughout this book. It all boils down to one simple idea. If you focus on this one concept, your Internet marketing practically takes care of itself.

Conversations Are Markets

If you want to access a particular market, you need to participate in the conversation surrounding that market. By participating in the conversation, you're engaging that community and becoming known within it. It all starts with awareness. Awareness leads to interest, and interest leads to demand. If they don't know you exist, that's where it ends. By linking to other bloggers and content providers (Chapter 40), you are engaging in the conversation. Those other bloggers will see that you exist and they will start to be aware of your thoughts and insights. By subscribing to other top bloggers in your field (Chapter 41), you will stay current with the conversation. Knowing what these thought-leaders are blogging about will give you an opportunity to chime in with your own perspective and expertise. By contacting and interviewing those very same thought-leaders (Chapter 42), you will introduce yourself to them and help deliver their expertise to those searching for it. Doing so will position you as a conduit of thought leadership in your industry. And by submitting your posts to blog carnivals (Chapter 43), you are once again engaging your community and contributing to the conversation.

But there's an even bigger opportunity. Not only can you *participate* in the conversation, but you can actually *facilitate* that conversation as well. Think about the people who built any of the large forums or bulletin boards on the Internet. Those people gain credibility by facilitating the conversation. Think about the people who built Facebook or Digg or Twitter. Think about Barack Obama and his 2008 campaign website hosting the blogs of more than 60,000 supporters. No matter your political affiliation, there's no disputing the fact that Obama's campaign website facilitated an enormous conversation, and he benefited as a result.

In the previous chapter, we talked about blog carnivals—how to post to carnivals in your field, host your own carnivals, and have other bloggers submit their posts to you. Hosting your own carnival is a great and simple way to begin facilitating the conversation in your field. All the active bloggers will quickly know you exist if you have your own carnival that you publish regularly. Installing a forum on your blog is another strategy. There are open source options in this area including Simple Machines, vBulletin, and others. If you have a substantial audience, a forum can quickly bring your online identity to the next level.

And of course, the standard blog functionality of allowing comments on your blog is another strategy to encourage the conversation. In fact, posting comments on other people's blogs is a great way to drive traffic to your website. (We'll talk more about that in Chapter 53.) People sometimes ask me if they should edit or delete derogatory comments on their blog. My answer is simple. Unless the comment is either spam or intentionally malicious, I would leave it up. Controversial comments are the best ones. They show you're being completely transparent. They prove you're authentic. And they encourage further dialogue among your followers. (See Chapter 28 for more information about negative comments.)

Any opportunity to foster interaction and communication among your users is good. And if the thought-leaders in your field start participating as well, your traffic could grow quickly. Conversations are markets. If you want to access a market on today's social Internet, participate in and facilitate the conversation. If you engage your community in an authentic way, you'll be amazed at the response you'll get.

Implementation Checklist

☐ Find the conversation in your field.
☐ Actively participate in the conversation.
☐ Facilitate the conversation if possible.
☐ Encourage the conversation to continue.
☐ Negative comments are not always bad.
☐ Authentic interactions build credibility.
☐ Compare notes and ideas with a colleague.

Chapter 45

Social Bookmarking

What is social bookmarking?

You might recognize website names such as Digg, Delicious, Reddit, and StumbleUpon—or maybe not! Either way, these platforms are playing an important role in the social media explosion revolutionizing today's Internet. Here's how they work. We're all familiar with "favorites." When you visit a website you like, you can bookmark it to your favorites, allowing you to quickly find the site again in the future. But what happens when you're using someone else's computer? You don't have access to your favorites anymore because they're on your computer, not the computer you're using.

Social bookmarking platforms are websites where you can create an account for yourself and then bookmark your favorites to that account rather than creating a bookmark on your computer. That means you'd have access to your favorites from any computer in the world. That's pretty neat, but it's a fairly basic piece of functionality. But wait! There's more.

The cool thing is that the social bookmarking platforms aggregate all the bookmarking activity of their users. What a wealth of information: Some of these platforms have more than 20 million users! That means you could go to Digg and search for tags such as "sports" or "news" and find the most bookmarked websites in the world about those topics. These results are found not through some complicated search engine algorithm, but according to your *peer group*. You could also search for "fly fishing in Alaska" or "sonatas by Mozart" or "mating habits of mosquitoes." In each case, you'll find the information your peer group is endorsing. What's important here is that your peer group is guiding your search, not a search engine. That's significant. It allows the peer group to educate itself. The peer group can evaluate content and reward the content it likes. It allows you to write a blog post and then bookmark it on the social bookmarking platforms, allowing your peer group to evaluate it for themselves. If they like it, their validation could catapult your post to a global audience within a few hours!

Every single day, blog posts get to the front page of Digg. Every day, someone's content is endorsed by the peer group, driving it up the rankings until it's at the very top. And every day, the posts that get to the top receive tens of thousands (or more) visitors from around the world. Is it easy to get to the top of Digg? No, it isn't. But is it possible? Yes. Social bookmarking delivers real-time democracy to its users. You can literally watch as good content rises and bad content fades. These platforms are changing the way people think. Back in the good old days, people looked at the *source* first and the *content* second. "Who are you?" came first. "What did you say?" came second.

Today, those questions have been reversed. Today, people look at the content first and the source second. It's a *big* change. That means good-quality content wins, even if it comes from a no-name blogger. If it's good-quality content, it's good-quality content. That's it. You don't need a fancy title or impressive credentials. All you need is good-quality content. And that represents an opportunity for all of us. The other social media platforms have the same basic functionality as the social bookmarking sites. You can "like" something on Facebook. You can "follow" someone on Twitter. You can "embed" someone's video from YouTube. In every case, members of the peer group are able to endorse each other's content.

This same cultural shift allowed an unknown community organizer to become President of the United States in eight short years. Think about how you can capitalize on this new dynamic. Pick your specialty. Stake your claim. Own your little piece of our information economy and demonstrate your expertise. If you provide real value with good-quality content, and if your content is validated by your peer group, the real-time democracy of today's social Internet will take care of the rest. When creating your blog, be sure to include all the social bookmarking buttons right on your website. Doing so reminds your readers to bookmark the page if they like it, and it's easier too. Each time you publish a new post, encourage your readers to bookmark it on the major platforms. Once your blog post is listed on those platforms, you pass the baton to your peer group and give the power to them. If your post provides real value, you never know where it might end up.

Implementation Checklist

- ☐ Visit Digg, Delicious, and StumbleUpon.
- ☐ Create an account for yourself on each.
- ☐ Search for your keywords on each platform.
- ☐ Notice which posts come up at the top.
- ☐ Watch what other users bookmark.
- ☐ Connect with members you agree with.
- ☐ Ensure your blog posts get bookmarked.
- ☐ Compare notes and ideas with a colleague.

Chapter 46

Online Branding

Want to be on the first page of Google?

Stupid question. Of course you do! The better question would ask *how* to get on the first page of Google results. Turns out, there are some websites that can quickly put your company right on the first page for searches in your local community, even if you don't have a website! These include Yelp, Citysearch, Yahoo! Local, MerchantCircle, and Google Places among others. Chapter 38 discussed niche directories that cater to specific verticals such as your industry or even your geographic location. Those directories can do an amazing job getting your name in front of qualified prospects, but they are less likely to show up on the front page of Google search results. Yahoo! Local, Citysearch, and Yelp are different. They don't necessarily attract hordes of Internet users who are all looking only for your particular service. On the contrary, they offer listings on a wide variety of topics, but they're such huge platforms that they rank high on the search engines.

Here's the strategy: First, visit all these websites and sign up for an account. By doing so, you're simply registering your existence in their data-bases. Then, once your account is created, get some of your past clients to write reviews of your business on those platforms. A client of mine was frustrated trying to get more clients online. We set up a Yelp account and started accumulating a few reviews. Now, when people search for his service (residential contracting) in his city, those Yelp reviews show up on the first page (his own website is on page four or five). (We'll discuss Yelp in more detail in Chapter 48.)

In fact, of the ten listings that come on the first page of Google search results, my client is mentioned in four of them! His listing on Yahoo! Local comes up (listing 4) followed by MerchantCircle (listing 5), Citysearch (listing 7), and Yelp (listing 9). Note that his own website is not listed on the first page, but his company nevertheless dominates the top search results.

On each of these platforms, make sure you fill out as much information as possible. Add descriptions and upload photos. If the platform allows you to connect with other users, reach out to other businesses. If the platform allows you to get reviews, promote that to your customers. The more complete your profile is, the better it will rank.

Search engine visibility is the biggest opportunity these websites provide. They're such large platforms that they almost always come up near the top of search results. Some are free. Others charge a fee but the online visibility is well worth the investment. Most people believe the only way to show up on Google is to have an incredible website that is perfectly optimized for the search engines. That's not true. There are other ways—strategies that are more effective and less expensive than trying to build a huge website all on your own (or hiring someone else to do it).

The easiest way to find these large localized directory sites is to search for your industry keywords and look at the domain names at the bottom of each search result listing. By looking at the URL as well as the description text, you can usually identify the platforms that host profiles for your competitors. Start by looking for listings with Yelp, Citysearch, or Yahoo! in the URL. Those will give you a good idea of the usual structure, making it easy to find other websites you can target as well. I recommend doing this every month or so, just to make sure you're taking advantage of all the opportunities available in your industry.

These are simple strategies that only take a few hours to pursue. The best part is that you can easily see what your competition is doing, just by looking at the search results in your field. By consistently targeting all the platforms others are using, you'll quickly populate the Internet with positive citations of your business. That exposure can bring you the customers you're looking for. Another advantage is that these websites get indexed by Google regularly. That means you can start seeing results quickly. I recently created a page on MerchantCircle and found the listing on Google within 30 minutes.

Get started! Done properly, this strategy can get you on the first page of Google search results in short order.

Implementation Checklist

☐ Create an account on Yahoo! Local.

☐ Create an account on Google Places.

☐ Create an account on Yelp.

☐ Create an account on MerchantCircle.

☐ Consider an account on Citysearch ($$).

☐ Search for your keywords on Google.

☐ Look for platforms others are using.

☐ Ask past clients to write reviews for you.

☐ Continue checking for new platforms.

☐ Compare notes and ideas with a colleague.

Chapter 47

Optimize Google Places

Is your business listed on Google Places?

What's Google Places? Well, if you search for something on Google, quite often you'll find a map at the top of the search results with upside-down red teardrop-shaped icons all over it (labeled A, B, C, etc.). And right beside that map, you'll find seven businesses listed, corresponding to the teardrops. That's Google Places. It's also been referred to as Google Local. The idea is to show relevant businesses that match search queries for local businesses, and also to show exactly where those businesses are located. But what happens if there are more than seven businesses that are relevant? What determines which businesses show up first, second, and third?

Google uses an algorithm to determine the order in which the businesses are listed. The Google Places algorithm is not the same as the algorithm for regular search results but it's an algorithm nonetheless. That means you now have to optimize your business for two Google algorithms, not one. First, you have to optimize your website for placement in regular search results—this is called search engine optimization (SEO), which we covered in Chapters 29, 30, 31 and 32. Second, you have to optimize your business for placement in the Google Places results, which is the subject of this chapter.

We'll start by reviewing the three criteria for the Google Places algorithm that Google has identified publicly: location, relevance, and prominence.

- *Location:* If the searcher includes a location name in the search query, Google will look for listings closest to that location. If no location is entered, Google will look for listings closest to the location of the searcher (determined by analyzing the Internet protocol—or IP—address of the searcher).
- *Relevance:* Based on the keywords entered into the search query, Google will look for the most relevant listings. Relevance is determined by the title of your business listing in Google Places and the description. (We'll look at this more closely later in the chapter.)
- *Prominence:* Google will present the most prominent listings first. For museums, as an example, Google knows which museums are most prominent. But what about small businesses? There's an opportunity here, so keep reading!

Let's talk about the tricks to gaining better placement in Google Places results. Let's say you own an Italian restaurant named simply "Mario's." You'd be much better off adding a couple more keywords to your Company/Organization name. For example, "Mario's Italian Pizzeria." Those keywords will help you rank for searches including "Italian" and/or "pizzeria." If you add keywords to your Company/Organization name on Google Places, be sure to update your website and other online listings with the same keywords. Google likes consistency. You may even wish to file a DBA (doing business as) at your local county clerk's office to make it official. As long as your keywords are consistent among your various online listings, the extra keywords will definitely help your ranking in Google Places.

You can't do much with your address. It is what it is. And I strongly discourage getting PO boxes in different cities to artificially accumulate duplicate references of your business. If you legitimately have offices in different locations, fine; include them all in your Google Places listing. (If you have only one location and would like to enhance your online reach, refer to Chapter 31 for a better approach.)

Make sure your listing in Google Places is complete. In particular, check that you're in the right category. Fill in all the hours-of-operation and payment information and write a good keyword-rich description. Upload pictures and videos if possible. Google likes complete listings. Build a big online presence. Google looks at citations of your business across the Internet as a gauge of your prominence. Make sure all the citations have the same business address and phone number. Although we talk about many strategies to build online exposure in this book, publishing articles online (Chapter 52) might be the fastest way to get a lot of citations quickly. Get reviews and ratings. Google is trying to push into the review business. They want to beat Yelp at their own game. If you have a bunch of good reviews, that will contribute to a better ranking. As with Yelp, you won't benefit with Google Places by accumulating fake reviews. Doing that is asking for trouble.

Google is tight-lipped about their algorithms, and for good reason. They don't want people manipulating the system. It's impossible to know exactly what the impact of the above suggestions will be, but they'll all play a small role in getting you to the top of the Google Places list. More than anything else, build the most complete business listing you can. It benefits everyone.

Implementation Checklist

- [ ] Create an account on Google Places.
- [ ] Try to incorporate keywords in your title.
- [ ] Ensure your title is consistent elsewhere.
- [ ] Fill out as much information as possible.
- [ ] Upload photos and videos where possible.
- [ ] Accumulate reviews from past clients.
- [ ] Build a massive online identity.
- [ ] Compare notes and ideas with a colleague.

Chapter 48

Leverage Yelp for Business

Do you have reviews on Yelp?

If you own a restaurant, the odds are good that you do. And certainly, if you live in a major metropolitan area like New York, Los Angeles, Chicago, or San Francisco, the odds are even higher. But for many businesses, the answer is *no*. It's time to change that. For those who don't know, Yelp is a review site that allows people to document their experiences with local businesses using a five-star scale and an area for written comments. It has become extremely popular in parts of the country, to the extent that a business's success or failure can be directly affected by its ratings on Yelp.

Yelp caters to local businesses. Restaurants, pubs, coffee shops, dry cleaners, dentists, massage therapists, chiropractors, hotels, gyms, and retail stores are all reviewed on Yelp. Yelp is also chasing the hot new "check-in" trend, following the success of the Foursquare mobile application. Foursquare allows people to "check-in," using their mobile phones, at local businesses, documenting their patronage in the process. The application is quite playful, allowing users to win "badges" and even become the "mayor" of particular businesses they frequent. Hoping to get in on the fun—and the growing popularity of the trend—Yelp has introduced check-in as well. In fact, Facebook recently introduced Facebook Places (Chapter 74) that has check-in functionality too and even Google has suggested they might join the party down the road.

The interesting thing about Yelp is how well it ranks on Google. Yelp is very well optimized for the search engines, so reviews posted on Yelp can easily show up on the first page of Google when people search for a particular business's name or keywords mentioned in the review.

What does that mean? It means you can be on the first page of Google without even having a website! This is what online branding is all about. It's about building a presence on high-ranking websites to expand your online identity. (Refer to Chapter 46 for more information about online branding.) Business owners can "claim" their businesses on Yelp. If you don't have a review yet, you simply create a profile for your business. But if you already have reviews (a lot of businesses already have reviews on Yelp without even knowing about them), you can *claim* the business and verify yourself as the business owner (or authorized representative).

They'll call your phone number or send you something in the mail and, once verified, you can edit the business information, upload photos, and reply to reviews. If you haven't already done so, visit Yelp and make sure your business is listed and you're verified. Similar to Google Places (Chapter 47), you'll want to fill in as much information as possible. Upload photos and include a description. You can also add a lot of specific business information including payment methods accepted, hours of operation, facility characteristics (like patios), and parking options. Fill it all out. All of these data points are searchable and if they're not included, you won't show up for users searching for those specifics.

Being verified with Yelp also allows you to reply to reviews. This is key. The rule of thumb: reply to as many reviews as you can, especially the bad ones. (Refer to Chapter 28 for more on negative comments.) Don't get mad. Don't freak out. Instead, thank the complainer for the comment and explain what you intend to do to rectify the situation. Keep in mind that people who are active on Yelp are among your most valuable customers. Not only are they more engaged in the consumer experience but they're sharing their experiences with their peer group. These people are influencers within your target market. Do whatever it takes to keep them happy. It's worth it.

Yelp allows businesses to post coupons and discounts on their profiles. Take advantage of this. Some of your customers look on Yelp before *and* after they interact with you. They might be looking at some of your competitors and deciding who they'll use based on reviews and coupons. Don't miss that opportunity. If you're hosting upcoming special events, post them on Yelp—you'll attract your ideal customers to your business. (Think about how you can engage your customers and prospects at fun events and refer to Chapter 59 for ideas on event promotion.)

Incidentally, when Yelp first got started, they had a hard time building a user base. After trying several marketing campaigns, they started holding parties for "elite Yelpers" in the San Francisco area. Those parties became *the* place to see and be seen for Silicon Valley trailblazers, and the parties quickly became Yelp's primary marketing strategy. Done properly, events are a highly effective way to engage your community! Add a Yelp badge to your website or blog. Yelp is a recognized review site. Not only will your business look more transparent and progressive but the badge will also encourage your website visitors to check out your reviews and possibly write one themselves. The more reviews you get, the more your Yelp profile will get found by active "Yelpers."

Integrate your Yelp account with Facebook and Twitter. Click "My Account" and then "External Services" to set up the configuration. Once complete, your reviews on Yelp will automatically be published on your Facebook wall and your Twitter feed. Being an active Yelper is a position of power. So don't restrict your participation to that of a business owner. Write reviews yourself. Connect with others. Once you have a few dozen friends and 50+ reviews, you'll appreciate both sides of the Yelp community and that will only enhance your participation as a business.

Implementation Checklist

- ☐ Make sure your business is listed on Yelp.
- ☐ Get verified as the business owner.
- ☐ Fill in as much information as possible.
- ☐ Upload photos and add descriptions.
- ☐ Reply to all reviews, good or bad.
- ☐ Post coupons and discounts on Yelp.
- ☐ Post your upcoming events on Yelp.
- ☐ Integrate Yelp with Facebook and Twitter.
- ☐ Write reviews for other businesses.
- ☐ Compare notes and ideas with a colleague.

Part Five

Attract Qualified Prospects

Chapter 49

Understand the Process

How do you drive traffic to your website?

This section of the book (this chapter and the next twelve) is devoted to answering that question. There are tons of different strategies to attract qualified prospects but we'll focus on some of the traditional traffic strategies in this section. The next section is all about social media. Before we get started, we have to introduce the Internet marketing process in general. And in its most basic form, Internet marketing is a very simple process.

Figure 49.1 breaks the Internet marketing process down to just two primary steps: get people to your website . . . and impress them once they get there. Simple. Two basic steps. A good portion of this book has dealt with the second step and it's worth noting that this step can be broken down further into two parts: Build trust first and then monetize that trust second. Nobody is going to buy anything from you unless they trust you first. I've repeated this throughout this book and it's critically important. Build trust! But without traffic, even *that* doesn't matter!

This section deals with the first step: driving traffic. Let's look at the process from a conceptual perspective. Essentially, the idea is to populate the Internet with valuable demonstrations of your expertise along with links back to your website. We want to show people how great you are and then

Understanding the Internet Marketing Process		
Get people to your website . . .	*. . . and impress them once they get there.*	
Drive Traffic	**Provide Value**	**Monetize Trust**

FIGURE 49.1   The Internet Marketing Process

give them a way to learn more. You live in a home. Your home has one front door. That's not the case for your website. Your website can have hundreds or even thousands of front doors. Any place that has a link to your website represents another front door. It's one more way to enter your website.

The idea behind driving traffic to your website is to put an attractive front door right in the middle of a huge crowd of your ideal customers. Figure out where they're browsing the Internet and then demonstrate your expertise right in front of them, and provide a link to your website. This process contributes to your SEO objectives as well because it adds more inbound links to your website, increasing your Google PageRank score.

You can think about it like fishing. You want to throw some tasty bait into a "raging river." I use this analogy a lot. A raging river is a website with *tons* of traffic. The tasty bait is your demonstration of expertise. (An astute editor once told me this analogy isn't technically accurate, that fast-running water would pull the bait off the hook—*not* something you'd want to happen. My apologies to any fishing experts out there if the analogy doesn't ring true, but I like the river and bait components, so I'm using it anyway!)

By the way, you need both. If you put great bait in a small stream, you won't get anything. If you throw rotten bait into a raging river, you will again get nothing. But if you find a combination of great bait and raging rivers, you'll hit the jackpot and can repeat the same process over and over again. This process implies two parts. First, you have to find raging rivers full of your ideal customers. There's no sense promoting a senior living facility on Myspace. It's the wrong audience. Myspace would be a better place to promote dating sites, music bands, or video games.

Second, you have to refine your bait to make it as appetizing and enticing as possible. Once you've found your target market, you have to demonstrate your expertise such that your audience wants to learn more. The next few chapters introduce some powerful strategies but the process is the same for almost any campaign. Even pay-per-click or banner advertisements follow the same basic model. You're promoting your value on a busy website in an enticing way, and providing a link. It's all the same.

Implementation Checklist

- ☐ Find your ideal customers on the Internet.
- ☐ Identify raging rivers where they browse.
- ☐ Demonstrate your expertise on those sites.
- ☐ Make sure your "bait" is super enticing.
- ☐ Give them a link to learn more about you.
- ☐ Repeat the process over and over again.
- ☐ Compare notes and ideas with a colleague.

Chapter 50

E-mail Marketing

How many people are on your e-mail list?

In Chapter 23, we discussed using your intermediate content to build an e-mail list. Have you started? How many people do you have so far? Did you set up your autoresponder? I hope so. And maybe you already have hundreds or even thousands of people on that list. If so, congratulations!

E-mail marketing is one of the most powerful tools for modern businesses. Not only can you deliver messages with absolutely zero delivery costs but you can contact your audience multiple times, establishing trust as you go. This book started as an e-mail course run through an autoresponder. Those who subscribed received one e-mail tip every week for a year. So there were 52 e-mails in all. The beauty is that those e-mails were all sent automatically. I wrote them at the beginning and uploaded them to the platform. After that, they got sent out according to a predetermined time-lapse schedule.

That means that while one person was receiving e-mail 19, another person might have been receiving e-mail 2 or e-mail 49. The timing was preset and didn't require any direct involvement from me. As long as the e-mails were written and uploaded, my job was done. At the same time, the people on my list got the information in the correct order and on a predictable schedule. Have you ever heard of the Rule of Seven? It says that people need to see your message seven times before they remember it and recognize you. In the good old days, that meant you had to send your audience seven direct mail pieces or hit them with seven marketing messages before you could expect respectable results. Today, it means you have to send seven e-mails before they start trusting you.

E-mail autoresponders are the perfect tool to build that trust. This chapter started out as the 18th tip in the e-mail course. By this point, recipients already knew a lot more about Patrick Schwerdtfeger than they did at the beginning. They knew the type of information they were getting as well as the strategies I espouse. You can obviously use an autoresponder for your marketing as well. Think about your business and what value you could push to your audience. Pretend you're a teacher and your prospects are your students. What can you teach them? How can you benefit their lives? Start writing an outline of all the lessons you'd like to cover.

You don't need to have all your lessons written by the time you launch the program. Do you think I had all 52 e-mails written when I first accepted subscriptions on my website? Absolutely not. I only had two e-mails written at that point! The rest I wrote later. I only needed to stay ahead of the first subscriber (which was me!) to keep the process seamless. Here's a good analogy. Maybe you've heard this one before. Here goes. If you and a friend are in the woods and you're both being chased by a bear, you really don't need to run faster than the bear. You only need to run faster than your friend. As long as you run faster than your buddy, you're in good shape! Yes, I know. It's a bit harsh. But it makes the point.

It's the same for an e-mail autoresponder. Don't worry about building the whole program before you launch. That's too much work. Instead, create your outline and write the first two or three e-mails. Then, reserve some time for writing more each week, ensuring you're always ahead of that first subscriber. Before you know it, you'll have the whole thing done and can relax while your list continues to grow.

E-mail lists are powerful tools. When people have voluntarily subscribed to your e-mail list, you gain influence with them. The cast of the popular television show *Friends* earned $1 million each per episode during the last two seasons. Why? They had influence with an audience, thereby creating an opportunity for advertisers. The same is true for e-mail lists. If you have a list of 10,000 or 20,000 e-mail addresses, you have influence with a large audience. You have what everyone else wants. I know one Internet marketer who has more than 800,000 e-mail subscribers. A big e-mail list gives you the power to promote other people's products and get a generous commission on the sale.

Remember Chapter 9? We talked about joint ventures and large e-mail distribution lists. With an e-mail autoresponder, you can build a list of your own and then provide endorsements for others who are trying to promote their products or services. In the case of information products (such as e-books, CDs, or DVDs), you can earn commissions as high as 50 percent or 75 percent of the product's sales price! That means you can earn a lot of money by endorsing other people's information products to your list. A large e-mail list is a valuable asset and one that can make you a fortune online. Although there are dozens of e-mail marketing platforms available, the three leading providers are Constant Contact, Infusionsoft, and aWeber. I used aWeber for the e-mail course. Check it out, and see if you can incorporate this powerful Internet marketing tool into your own business.

Implementation Checklist

- ☐ Pretend you're a teacher with expertise.
- ☐ Pretend your prospects are your students.
- ☐ Think about the lessons you could deliver.
- ☐ Create an outline for a series of lessons.
- ☐ Write out the first two or three lessons.
- ☐ Visit aWeber and Constant Contact first.
- ☐ Visit Infusionsoft and research that as well.
- ☐ Google "e-mail autoresponders" to compare.
- ☐ Decide which platform you'd like to use.
- ☐ Upload the initial lessons to your account.
- ☐ Create a sign-up web form (easy to do).
- ☐ Put the sign-up form on your website.
- ☐ Promote your program to get subscribers.
- ☐ Compare notes and ideas with a colleague.

Chapter 51

Start a Podcast

Are you featured on the iTunes Music Store?

Although I have always been fascinated with technology, I effectively got my start by creating a podcast series called "Beyond the Rate," which was about the mortgage business, and posting it on iTunes. That was back in 2006 and at one point "Beyond the Rate" was the third most popular mortgage-related podcast on iTunes. Like so many other websites we've discussed in this book, iTunes is a raging river. It's an online destination with tons of traffic. It's a perfect place to demonstrate your expertise. Millions of people look for things on iTunes. Yes, most of them are searching for music but some are searching for information too.

Similar to the way people can subscribe to your blog, they can also subscribe to your podcast. Once subscribed, they will automatically be notified when you upload your next podcast episode. In fact, if they're subscribed through iTunes, your latest episode will automatically download every time they log in. Most podcasts are in audio format and a significant percentage of people listen to your content on their MP3 player when they're either commuting to work, getting some exercise at the gym, or walking their dog.

It's common knowledge that people give more credence to a statement if it's accompanied by a photo. This is why testimonials commonly include photos of the person along with his or her words. When people can see a photo, the words become real. Readers identify with the message more quickly.

The trust-instilling effect of audio and video is even greater than that of still photographs. Photos are trusted more than basic text. Audio content is trusted more than photos and video is trusted most of all. The easier it is for them to *identify* with the source, the easier it is for them to trust the source.

151

And as we all know, people have to trust you before they'll be willing to buy anything. With audio podcasts, your listeners hear your voice and the tonality of your delivery. It's way more personal than a typed blog post. I've had people call me and be amazed that they're *actually* speaking with me, after having listened to my podcasts beforehand.

Creating audio content has never been easier. You need little more than a decent microphone and some recording software. Thankfully, the software is free. For Mac users, it's called GarageBand; for PC users, there are several options but I recommend Audacity. You can download and install Audacity in seconds, just by entering "audacity recording software" in a Google search. I recommend spending a few dollars on the microphone. They range in price from about $10 to $600. I'm not suggesting you need to spend $600 but I do recommend getting something in the $50 range. The difference in sound quality is noticeable.

There are three other things you'll need. First, pick up a stand for your new microphone. It's worth the money. It keeps the microphone steady while you deliver your message and that helps to keep your recording volume even throughout your message. Second, you absolutely *must* get a "pop filter." What's that? It looks like a large foam rubber ball that fits on the top of your microphone. Without it, your P's, B's, and D's pop into the microphone and later pop into the listeners' ears. It's distracting. Hold the palm of your hand up to your mouth and say the word "podcast." You'll feel the air hit your hand when you say *p*. Without the foam rubber to divert that air, the microphone picks it up as a loud pop. You can buy a pop filter for less than $10 and it will eliminate those pops. Third, you'll need an RSS hosting account. It's an online account where you can upload your MP3 files, allowing people to download them from iTunes and dozens of other "podcast directories." It'll cost you less than $10 per month. There are several RSS hosting options, but I have my account with Libsyn.

Regardless which service you use, the initial configuration process can be a bit complicated, but once that's done, you can upload new podcasts and have iTunes (and all the other podcast directories you registered with) updated automatically. When you record your podcasts, I recommend that you use audio effects such as compression and bass boost to improve the sound quality. I used both on my own recordings and they round out my voice and make it sound smooth and buttery, like a radio announcer!

Podcasting is another strategy that requires consistency to succeed. Frankly, I missed my own opportunity. I did an introduction, 15 chapters, and a conclusion. That was it. I stopped. Stupid. I was just hitting my stride.

I should've kept going and become a "real estate guru." In hindsight, I'm happy to be out of the real estate business (for obvious reasons) but it's an important point. Consistency wins. If you start a podcast and do it long enough, you'll end up with a loyal and growing audience. And that can fuel your business far into the future.

Implementation Checklist

- ☐ Consider starting an audio podcast.
- ☐ Buy a $50 microphone to start recording.
- ☐ Get a stand and a $10 pop filter as well.
- ☐ Mac users: use GarageBand.
- ☐ PC users: download and install Audacity.
- ☐ Get an RSS hosting account.
- ☐ Pick a topic and record your first podcast.
- ☐ Use compression and bass boost effects.
- ☐ Register your podcast with iTunes.
- ☐ Register with podcast directories as well.
- ☐ Record and upload new episodes regularly.
- ☐ Compare notes and ideas with a colleague.

Chapter 52

Publish Articles Online

Would you like your articles to be published on high traffic websites?

Of course you would. This chapter is about publishing educational articles online. Not only does this strategy drive targeted traffic to your website, but it also builds credibility and positions you as an expert in your field. To start the process, write an article demonstrating your expertise. It doesn't have to be long, just 500 to 700 words. Once the article is complete, there are many online article directories where you can publish your article along with an Author Resource Box where you can plug your website and include a link. One such directory is iSnare.com; this platform also provides an article distribution service. For less than $2, iSnare will distribute your article to literally thousands of different article directories.

It makes sense to understand the revenue model of these article directories. They want as many articles as they can get and they line the sides of their website with "Ads by Google," hoping readers click on the ads. If they do, the article directory gets a small commission. The moral of the story is that they don't really care if your article is good or not. They just want the content. In other words, you don't have to be a recognized expert to get "published" on these directories. They'll take articles from anyone (as long as it's not sexually explicit, hate material, or other objectionable content).

In 2007, I did an experiment and published 70 articles in 70 days. By the end of the 70 days, a Google search for "Patrick Schwerdtfeger" (I have a pretty unusual last name!) brought up more than 90,000 results. That means my articles had been published in 90,000 different places, each with a link back to my website. The process had added 90,000 front doors to my website! Imagine the credibility I get when someone Googles my name and sees thousands of results, each referencing me as the "expert author" of one article or another.

Be sure to include a call to action, either within your articles or in the Author Resource Box. When people find your articles, you want them to be so impressed with your knowledge that they click on your link and end up back on your website. Give them a reason. Tell readers that you have additional resources on your blog. Tell them about your intermediate content (Chapter 23). These articles are part of your beginner content (Chapter 22) and they all need to point back to the next level in your sales funnel.

The other nice thing about article marketing is that the articles stay out there for a long time, generating traffic to my website month after month. More than a year after my test, I was still getting traffic from those articles. By the way, I said earlier that the distribution service costs less than $2. The truth is that it costs one "credit" to distribute one article. If you buy only a few credits, they cost about $1.80 each; but if you buy in larger volume, the credits cost less than $1. Knowing I was going to publish a lot of articles, I bought a lot of credits. So the whole exercise cost me less than $70.

One article directory, EzineArticles.com (discussed in earlier chapters), dominates the category. More than 80 percent of my article marketing traffic came from this one website. iSnare does *not* distribute to EzineArticles so you have to upload your articles manually . . . but it's worth it.

www.ezinearticles.com

If you plan to publish articles to build credibility and drive traffic to your website, be sure to include EzineArticles.com in your campaign. Not only is it a great platform, but it also provides unparalleled statistics about the number of people reading your articles and how many clicked on the links in your Author Resource Box at the bottom of each article. (As mentioned in Chapter 30, the words that carry these links to your website are called "anchor text" and are included in the search engine algorithms.) When publishing articles, you can write your own Author Resource Box and put the link on any words you choose. That represents a great opportunity to boost your website's ranking for your primary keyword phrase. Populate the Internet with your expertise, establish credibility, drive traffic to your website, and improve your search engine ranking, all at the same time.

Implementation Checklist

☐ Write articles of 500 to 700 words.
☐ Write educational articles, not promotional.
☐ Write an Author Resource Box with a link.
☐ Put the link on your primary keywords.
☐ Point the link to your website.
☐ Mention your intermediate content.
☐ Always include a call to action.
☐ Upload your articles to EzineArticles.com.
☐ Distribute your articles on iSnare.com.
☐ Compare notes and ideas with a colleague.

Chapter 53

Post on Blogs and Forums

What's the most immediate traffic-generating strategy?

I've tested a lot of different things and the most immediate strategy by far is posting on popular online forums. So what's a forum? Let's start with a definition. Forums are essentially places where online conversations take place. Each individual conversation is called a "thread." Members of the forum can start a thread by asking a question or making a statement. Then other members can enter the thread and provide an answer or contribute their thoughts about the original statement. Soon, the thread grows to include contributions from multiple members, each attempting to demonstrate their expertise. You see, they're all using the forum to drive traffic to their own websites, just like you and me. And because they all want to impress each other with their knowledge and insights, forums are among the best places to *learn* about your field.

When you become a member of a forum, you create a profile for yourself including links to your website. In some cases, you can even create a signature similar to an e-mail signature. Every time you contribute to a thread and demonstrate your expertise, your signature appears immediately below your comments. That signature can include a link to your website. The idea is to contribute some useful information or insights to the conversation, enticing other members to click through to your own website. Remember, every link is another "front door" to enter your website and learn more about you.

Popular forums often have thousands of active threads going at one time. Every time someone adds a comment to a particular thread, it moves to the very top of the list. Then, when someone adds a comment to a different thread, the first thread moves down one notch and the second thread takes its place at the top of the list. Obviously, the threads at the top of the list get the most traffic. I call that the "fast water" and you want your contributions to be in the fast water as much as possible. Contributing to the most active threads is a good strategy. Not only will your contribution push the thread to the top of the list, but other people's contributions will keep it up there after you're gone.

As I said at the beginning, this strategy has the most immediate impact on your website's traffic. It works fast. You can create an account on a popular forum, post some comments on active threads, and see referral traffic on your website within an hour.

How can you find popular forums in your field? There are two easy ways. First, visit Big-Boards and do a search for your keywords. It lists the biggest forums in your area. (We first introduced Big-Boards back in Chapter 7 when we were trying to find your target market.)

http://directory.big-boards.com

Second, do a search in Google for your keywords plus the word "forum." You can rest assured that whatever comes up at the top is a high-traffic forum. You can also search for "forum directory" to find additional suggestions.

Most online forums keep track of the number of contributions you've made and that statistic becomes a measure of your credibility and activity level within the community. As a result, your contributions won't get as much attention when you have only a few posts as they will when you have lots of posts. Once you've accumulated a reasonable number of posts (more than 100 for example), try starting your own thread. The top comments within a thread are seen the most. If you initiate the thread yourself, your initial comments are always at the top of that thread.

Ask an interesting question. Offer a list of resources. Make a provocative statement. You want your thread to become active. You want other forum members to see your thread and want to contribute. Never overpromote yourself. That will repel other forum members. Instead, provide value. Contribute something useful. If you succeed, you'll be in the fast water longer and that will drive more traffic to your website. A lot of people sustain their entire business on forums. I spend a lot of time on the Warrior Forum (the largest forum about Internet marketing) and some members have more than 8,000 posts. Comments from those members are worth gold and they build impressive fan bases as a result.

Blogs are another great place to post comments. In fact, the ability for readers to post comments is one of the primary characteristics of blogs. Again, you can include a link along with your comment. The trick is to find the blog posts that rank high for your keywords and then make your contributions there. As we've discuss in previous chapters, two great places to search for popular blogs include Technorati and Google BlogSearch.

www.technorati.com

http://blogsearch.google.com

Visit them both. Search for your keywords. Find popular blog posts that rank high on the search engines. Read those posts and contribute your own thoughts to the conversation. If your comments provide real value, other readers will click on your link to learn more about you. Blogs and forums offer great opportunities to drive traffic to your website. Be part of the conversation. Demonstrate your expertise. Provide value. The rest takes care of itself.

Implementation Checklist

- ☐ Search Big-Boards.com for your keywords.
- ☐ Use Google to find big forums in your field.
- ☐ Get an account and build your profile.
- ☐ Read a few threads before writing anything.
- ☐ Select threads where you can contribute.
- ☐ Provide value to the conversation.
- ☐ Never overpromote. It's tacky.
- ☐ Start your own value-based threads.
- ☐ Search for popular blogs in your field.
- ☐ Post comments with a link to your website.
- ☐ Demonstrate your expertise, provide value.
- ☐ Compare notes and ideas with a colleague.

Chapter 54

Post on Yahoo! and Amazon

How can you leverage Yahoo! and Amazon?

There are easy ways to do both. Let's start with Yahoo! Chapter 53 talked about posting comments on popular blogs and forums. The idea was to demonstrate your expertise right in front of a huge crowd of your ideal customers, enticing them to visit your website. One of the largest forums on the Internet is Yahoo! Answers. Users either ask questions or provide answers. You can find just about every question you can imagine on Yahoo! Answers. If you're ever curious about something, check there first. In most cases, you'll get the answers you need.

The interesting thing about Yahoo! Answers is that users can rate the answers provided by others. The answer with the most votes is labeled as the best answer and the person who provided the answer is given credit. In fact, every answer is accompanied by a note stating how many "best answers" that person has provided. This feature lends serious credibility to those who provide good information. After all, these answers are all being evaluated within the peer group. This transparency creates a tremendous opportunity for those who contribute real value to their community. The way the platform is structured allows people with true expertise to rise to the top and get acknowledged for the value they provide. If you have true expertise, you can benefit from that process.

Yahoo! Answers is a huge platform with massive traffic. The people who are well established on Yahoo! Answers have a steady stream of ideal customers knocking at their door. Think about it. Who would find your answers? The only people who would find your contributions are those who are searching for the questions you provided answers to. The only people who would find you are precisely those who need your expertise.

That's the most fascinating thing about the Internet. Unlike the offline world, you can target your ideal customer with incredible precision. By selecting the questions you have answers to, you are automatically segmenting the market to only those who need your knowledge.

Let's talk about Amazon. Most people know Amazon as an online book seller even though the site sells much more than books. But let's focus on books for now. When you look for books on Amazon, you can read the reviews of others who have read them before you. Many people rely on those reviews more than the regular product description. Well, you can write those reviews just like anyone else.

Once again, the process allows for precision targeting. Who will find you? The only people who will find you are those who are considering the book you have already read—the people who want the knowledge you already have. By writing reviews for popular books in your field, you are demonstrating your expertise to your ideal customers.

Like Yahoo! Answers, Amazon has tons of traffic—millions of unique visitors each month. Writing reviews is a great way to demonstrate your expertise in the middle of a raging river, full of prospects you can target with precision.

On both platforms—Yahoo! and Amazon—there are ways to point people to your website. On Yahoo! Answers, you can put a link to your website in your profile description. It's a little harder on Amazon. They have removed the ability to add live links in your profile but you can include your URL in your profile name. That puts your website address right beside every review you write.

You'll find that some of these strategies match your needs better than others. Select the ones that work well with your business model and your expertise. Within each strategy, there are people who sustain their entire businesses by mastering that particular technique. You can do it too.

Implementation Checklist

- ☐ Visit Yahoo! Answers and get an account.
- ☐ Search for questions using your keywords.
- ☐ Read the questions people have asked.
- ☐ Read the answers people have contributed.
- ☐ Contribute your own expertise if possible.
- ☐ Don't post unless your answer is valuable.
- ☐ Find popular how-to books on Amazon.
- ☐ Read the reviews others have contributed.
- ☐ Create an account and include your URL.
- ☐ Write reviews for the best-selling books.
- ☐ Compare notes and ideas with a colleague.

Chapter 55

Online Classified Advertising

What's the ugliest website on the Internet? My vote goes to Craigslist!

Craigslist is one of the most basic websites imaginable. It's nothing more than a huge bulletin board. No graphics. No fancy colors. Just text links and hundreds of thousands of advertisements. But as of this writing, it's the 10th most popular website in America (according to Alexa). Craigslist is a raging river. It's an online destination with *tons* of traffic. The website boasts more than 50 million visitors self-publishing more than 30 million classified ads every month. Is there a way to leverage that traffic and gain some exposure? Absolutely. Let's take a look.

As you probably know, Craigslist posts the most recent ad at the top and all the other ads in reverse chronological order down the page. When you first post your ad, it's at the very top. But as soon as someone else posts a different ad in the same category, your ad drops down to second place. When a third person posts an ad, yours drops down to third place, and so on. Obviously, the ads at the top get the most traffic. Similar to forums, that's the "fast water." When your ad drops down 100 spots or more, you're on the second page and your exposure drops off dramatically. If you want to stay in the fast water, you need to post new ads as often as possible.

The interesting thing about Craigslist is that they don't allow you to post the same ad on consecutive days. In fact, they have a seven-day rotation. That means you can run the same ad every Monday or every Tuesday but not more often than that. Turns out, that's good news. If you want to post new ads on Craigslist once each day, you need to write different versions to avoid the duplicate ad restrictions. Well, the process of writing different versions of your ad actually forces you to test different wording. To be clear, different versions of your ad have to be *substantially* different to avoid the duplicate ad restrictions. You can't just change the title and a few words here and there. You really have to write entirely unique ads.

Testing is at the heart of Internet success. You have to test to see what generates good results and what does not. Craigslist forces you to test your ad copy and that helps you improve your message. You'll find that "discover" tests higher than "learn." "Free" tests higher than "cheap." It won't take long and you'll start seeing what works and what doesn't. You should also test the location of your ads. There are dozens of categories on Craigslist; each category attracts different users searching for different things. Some categories get very little traffic while others get heavy traffic. The Craigslist categories that get some of the heaviest traffic include "women looking for men" personals ads, employment ads, "apartments for rent" ads, and "cars for sale" ads.

Meanwhile, other categories get far less traffic. "Services" is a good example. This category is designed specifically for people who want to advertise their professional services—plumbers, real estate agents, lawyers, and insurance agents. Not surprisingly, there are tons of listings but not many visitors.

Get creative with your ad placement. Try different approaches in different categories to see which combination works best. Don't post to multiple categories at the same time. Instead, try one category one day and another category on a different day. Again, you'll need different versions to do so but you'll also reach different audiences in the process.

A past client does large scale commercial lending. He only does loans larger than $10 million. He earns an impressive income and his only advertising is on Craigslist. He posts two (entirely unique) ads every morning, Monday to Friday, and gets between five and ten inquiries per day. Not only has he tested different ad copy and different category placement but he has also tested different cities. Craigslist has more than 500 city platforms in more than 50 countries. Here in America, they have every major city covered. Because my former client can lend anywhere across the country, he tested different cities to see where he got the best results. Today, he only posts his ads in southern states such as Oklahoma, Arkansas, and Louisiana.

A woman who attended one of my presentations was a feng shui consultant. She told me that she once posted ads in the Gigs section of Craigslist. Because the Gigs section is similar to the employment listings, it gets a lot of traffic. The ad apparently asked homeowners to fill out a detailed survey about interior décor. Participants were paid $5 and all of the completed surveys were entered into a raffle for a complimentary feng shui consultation. Her ad got a good response and she promptly called each participant to inform them that they were the winner. Everyone won! After all, that's what she was looking for in the first place. Everyone won an in-person feng shui assessment in their own home. It gave her a perfect opportunity to demonstrate her expertise to her ideal customers and potentially get hired to adjust their interior décor along feng shui principles. She used Craigslist to build a list of highly targeted prospects for her service.

Allocate some time to write five different versions of an ad promoting your product or service. Run one each day and use Google Analytics (Chapter 33) to see which yields the worst response. Improve that particular ad and run all five ads again next week. Each week, improve the ad yielding the worst response. Doing so ensures you remain on a continuous improvement trajectory. Over time, your ads will get better and better, and you'll be well on your way to an effective Craigslist advertising campaign.

Implementation Checklist

- ☐ Search Craigslist for your keywords.
- ☐ Read the ads your competitors are posting.
- ☐ Notice which sections they are posting in.
- ☐ Write an advertisement for your business.
- ☐ Get creative with your approach and offer.
- ☐ Include either a link or accept e-mails.
- ☐ If using a link, use analytics to measure.
- ☐ Post your ad and measure the results.
- ☐ Write different versions of your ad.
- ☐ Test each ad to see which is most effective.
- ☐ Improve the worst performing ad weekly.
- ☐ Run ads regularly and monitor results.
- ☐ Compare notes and ideas with a colleague.

Chapter 56

Pay-Per-Click Advertising

Would you spend 50 cents to speak with a qualified prospect?

You'd be crazy not to. That's the cheapest sales strategy available! So what if you could pay the same price to bring someone to your website? Is that a good deal? If you've followed the advice in this book and built a website that speaks to its visitors and leads them down a path to provide value and build trust, it might just work. Pay-per-click (PPC) advertising allows you to display an advertisement to people who use search engines to search for specific keywords that you select. You can also position your PPC ads on related-content websites. If you sell Persian carpets, for example, you can select those words—"persian carpets"—and have your ad show up for precisely those people who are searching for that. Once again, unlike the offline world, you can target your audience with unparalleled accuracy.

The other cool thing about PPC advertising is that you only get charged if someone clicks on your ad and lands on your website. If they don't click, it doesn't cost a penny. The Google PPC program is called Google AdWords. Yahoo! and MSN offer similar programs but this chapter focuses on the Google AdWords program.

http://adwords.google.com

Does every click cost 50 cents? No. Some cost more and others cost less. This chapter explains the basics of the system and how it works. The cost to have your ad show up for a particular keyword phrase depends on how many people are competing for the same keyword phrase. It's similar to an auction. If the demand for that phrase is high, it costs more. If the demand is low, it costs less.

166

Here's the interesting thing. If you know what you're doing, you can find better qualified prospects for less money. Let me explain. Someone searching for the word "carpet" on Google is probably not a buyer. They don't know exactly what they're looking for. If they did, they would've used more words in their query. Searching for just one word is far too broad. They're probably just kicking tires.

Consider someone who searches for "antique silk Persian carpet." Now, that person is a buyer! And they proved it by entering four words into their Google search. They know exactly what they want and they're probably ready to buy. Which keyword phrase do you think has more competition: "carpet" or "antique silk Persian carpet?" You guessed it! The first phrase has more competition and costs far more than the second phrase. Meanwhile, the prospect searching for the first phrase is just kicking tires while the prospect searching for the second phrase is probably ready to buy. Most people who do PPC advertising pay far too much for their clicks because they're using short generic keyword phrases. If the person who sells Persian carpets selected that one-word keyword phrase, it would cost far more than if he or she selected a variety of longer, more descriptive phrases.

Consider the following keyword phrases:

- antique silk Persian carpet
- antique wool Persian carpet
- vintage silk Persian carpet
- vintage wool Persian carpet
- refurbished silk Persian carpet
- refurbished wool Persian carpet
- antique silk Persian rug
- antique wool Persian rug
- vintage silk Persian rug
- vintage wool Persian rug
- refurbished silk Persian rug
- refurbished wool Persian rug

If the seller of Persian rugs were to select these 12 descriptive keyword phrases (each having four words), the cost per click for his or her ads would be much lower than the cost per click for ads that targeted shorter, less descriptive keyword phrases. Also, the ads would display only for higher quality prospects.

By targeting "long tail" phrases (mentioned way back in Chapter 2), you'll attract better quality prospects for less money. As a reminder, the "long tail" refers to the exploitation of super specific niches on the Internet. A properly optimized Google AdWords campaign might target hundreds or even thousands of long tail keyword phrases. When you target longer phrases, you have to include every possible combination of words. I once optimized a client's Google AdWords campaign and increased the keyword phrases being targeted from just two to more than 400. But his average cost-per-click dropped from more than $3 per click to just 23 cents on average.

Start writing down some of the phrases you might like to target. Do some research (Chapter 13) and then write out all the possible combinations of the words you selected.

There's one more thing that helps determine how much you pay for a particular keyword phrase and that's your Quality Score. The Quality Score looks at the keywords you're targeting, the keywords in the actual ad, and the keywords on the "landing page." When someone clicks on your ad, the destination web page is referred to as the landing page. If the keywords are consistent throughout, you get a high Quality Score. If not, you get a low Quality Score. Obviously, Google doesn't want its AdWords clients to target high-traffic keywords to try and sell them something completely unrelated. That would frustrate users. So Google developed the Quality Score to ensure ads on the Google platform are relevant for users.

Ads with a high Quality Score pay far less than ads with a low Quality Score, so make sure your ads and landing page contain the same keywords you're targeting. The Google AdWords platform allows you to select a maximum bid per click and a daily budget for your campaign. That means you can limit your risk. And once you set up your campaign, the ads show up within 15 minutes. Sign up for an account. Give it a try, even if just for a week or two. It's fun and gets people to your website in a hurry!

Implementation Checklist

- ☐ Get an account with Google AdWords.
- ☐ Walk through the set-up process. It's easy.
- ☐ Write an ad to promote your business.
- ☐ Select keyword phrases to target.
- ☐ Use only three- or four-word keyword phrases.
- ☐ Select a maximum bid of 50 or 75 cents.
- ☐ Set a daily budget of $10 and give it a try.
- ☐ Explore the Google Keyword Selector Tool.
- ☐ Ensure you have a high Quality Score.
- ☐ Targeted keywords = keywords in your ad.
- ☐ Targeted keywords = keywords on your website.
- ☐ Play with the program and monitor results.
- ☐ Compare notes and ideas with a colleague.

Chapter 57

Write a Press Release

Have you ever sent out a press release?

If you're like most people who own small businesses, the answer is *no*. But the opportunity with public relations and press releases is growing, not shrinking. Back in the good old days, press releases were only intended for journalists and media coverage, but the Internet has changed that. Let's start the discussion by looking at today's marketing process.

Modern marketing can essentially be broken down into two stages. First, you have to market to people who do not yet know who you are. This is the process of finding, attracting, and qualifying prospects. Second, once a prospect has found you, you have to market to that prospect again, ensuring your company instills confidence with your audience. What do people do when they hear about you or your company? Many of them look you up on Google or one of the other search engines. Maybe not everyone does this, but many do, and that percentage is growing every year. Put your name or your company name into a Google search. What comes up? Anything? Good stuff? Bad stuff? Weird stuff?

When you send out a press release, you populate the Internet with information that you control. That's a tremendous opportunity. There are platforms that allow you to distribute press releases to a huge number of news-related websites. These are often referred to as "wire services" and one of my favorites is PRWeb.

www.prweb.com

PRWeb has four primary distribution options ranging from $80 to $360 and they put your news story on dozens of high-powered websites. So

170

what does that mean? It means your news story will show up all over the first few pages of any Google search about you. But the opportunity doesn't stop there. If you optimize your title and content with keywords, your news story could come up for many other searches as well. That means you can use press releases to market to people who already know you and also to those who do not know you yet. Here's the thing: many of these news providers have big powerful websites. That means they rank high on the search engines. The trick is to leverage those high rankings by positioning keyword-optimized news stories about you and your company on those websites.

Do this consistently and you can flood the Internet with positive stories about you, your company, and your keywords. Of course, the traditional public relations strategies still offer opportunities and we should spend some time talking about press releases and how to write stories that get picked up by the traditional media outlets. Chances are, your news story will never make the top headlines but that doesn't mean you won't get coverage. Think about the major news stories dominating the headlines today. Try to incorporate those headlines into your own story.

Media providers present the news in chunks. Watch your local news. You'll see for yourself. They almost always present three or four related stories at one time. The first one is usually the primary headline but two or three related stories often follow and that's the area you want to target with your press release.

Always think about what's going on in the world and try to piggy back on something the media outlets are already covering. There are lots of holidays during the year and days (or even weeks) devoted to one cause or another. These all represent opportunities for press releases. Try to incorporate all three of these strategies:

1. Include your name or the name of your company.
2. Optimize the release with targeted keywords.
3. Select an angle that incorporates a major news story.

Modern PR integrates all of these considerations and offers a wide variety of benefits. Don't let the opportunities pass you by. Write a press release. Test it. See what happens. It'll cost you $360 or less and might score you some valuable media publicity.

Implementation Checklist

- ☐ Write press releases about your company.
- ☐ Think about the big stories on the news.
- ☐ Incorporate those stories in press releases.
- ☐ Put your keywords in the title and content.
- ☐ Visit PRWeb and read about their services.
- ☐ Use a wire service to distribute releases.
- ☐ Compare notes and ideas with a colleague.

Chapter 58

Start a Group or Club

Can you be an effective group organizer?

You might surprise yourself. I did! Back in mid 2007, I stepped in as the organizer for an entrepreneur group on Meetup.com. The group had about 100 members at that time but they hadn't had an in-person meeting in months and the group was falling apart. At the time of this writing, my Meetup group has about 2,000 members and is one of the 50 largest entrepreneur clubs in the country. It's called the Entrepreneur and Small Business Academy and we've been sponsored by American Express OPEN, Microsoft, General Electric, and Hewlett-Packard at one time or another.

www.meetup.com/academy

The interesting thing is that I never invited a single member. They all found me! The Meetup platform hosts thousands of different groups and has millions of visitors each month. Many of those visitors are members of an existing group but they also browse through other groups that cater to their individual interests. Meetup isn't the only platform that supports groups. Yahoo! and Google both have platforms to organize groups. You can also start groups on Myspace, Facebook, and LinkedIn, among others. In each case, you can start a group and have people find you and join. I like Meetup the best because I think the viral effect is the strongest on that platform.

The reality is that most Meetup groups don't do very well. Their meetings are poorly attended and their membership growth is anemic. Meanwhile, my group has one primary meeting each month and we usually get between 100 and 200 people in attendance. I attribute the success of my group to the following three critical factors:

1. Content
2. Structure
3. Communication

- *Content:* Whether your group is exclusively online or has an offline component, provide your membership with quality content. Give them good useful information. That's what they want. If you consistently deliver value, your group will grow.
- *Structure:* Facilitate structured meetings. People like structure. They want to know exactly what to expect. Many leaders hate structure, but followers love it. Obviously, the distinction between leaders and followers depends on the situation, but the message is clear: groups with structure do better than those without it.
- *Communication:* Communication is critical. You need to keep your membership well informed about your activities as a group facilitator. Take a leadership role. Make decisions and tell your membership what's going on.

Meetup recently did a study and found that events with large descriptions (400 words or more) had better attendance than events with short descriptions. This is another angle to the communication element. Tell your members what to expect in detail. They'll appreciate it. You may or may not feel comfortable becoming a group organizer but the benefits are clear. Becoming an organizer put me at the center of the entrepreneur community in the San Francisco Bay Area. We have very productive meetings and most of our events are free. Our members receive clear value and that leaves me with tremendous social equity. People have done kind things for me and I count myself lucky to know such wonderful people. I use Google Analytics to monitor my website statistics and my group homepage on Meetup consistently refers quality traffic to my Tactical Execution blog. I get business from the group. I have found great resources in the group. I've made friends in the group. It's been a wonderful experience from the start.

Here's another angle. In June 2008, I bought a camcorder and started recording the presentations we have at our meetings. I post the videos on my YouTube channel, making the content available to a much broader audience.

www.youtube.com/tacticalexecution

The cool thing is that our meetings only take place once but the videos last forever! The videos become an annuity that I (and our speakers) benefit from long into the future. In fact, many speakers don't have any video footage, and they're grateful when I provide that for them. Some of my speakers have secured new business with people who found them on my YouTube channel. That makes me feel great and it attracts other high-quality speakers to my group. Meetup and YouTube make a great combination. It's changed my business and I hope it might one day change yours too.

Implementation Checklist

- ☐ Visit Meetup.com and search for keywords.
- ☐ See which groups exist and visit a few.
- ☐ Visit Yahoo! Groups and Google Groups.
- ☐ Search groups on Facebook and LinkedIn.
- ☐ See what other groups are doing.
- ☐ Consider starting your own group or club.
- ☐ Content: deliver value to your members.
- ☐ Structure: facilitate well-organized events.
- ☐ Communication: keep members informed.
- ☐ Become known within your community.
- ☐ Compare notes and ideas with a colleague.

Chapter 59

Event Marketing Strategies

Do you promote offline events?

Holding events is one of the best ways to grow your business. It positions you as the expert in your field and puts you in front of multiple prospects all at one time. My favorite word: leverage! As we discussed in Chapter 58, you can start a group or club on any number of platforms including Facebook, LinkedIn, Yahoo! Groups, Google Groups, and Meetup. But the challenge of actually promoting these events remains. Let's look at a few marketing strategies that can help drive registrations.

First, you may already know that you can post your events on a huge number of websites including Craigslist, WorkIt, Meetup, Plancast, and many local media websites. Problem: doing this is a major pain in the neck. Every platform has different submission requirements and online forms, not to mention the challenge of knowing all the relevant websites to begin with. As luck would have it, there's an online service that solves the problem. FullCalendar is a platform where you pay $19.95 and upload your event information just once and then have them populate dozens or even hundreds of other websites on your behalf.

www.fullcalendar.com

The FullCalendar service is available only in major U.S. cities (listed on their homepage) but if you happen to live in one of these cities, it's a great way to get the word out quickly and easily (and inexpensively). I once had an event in downtown San Francisco and marketed it *only* on FullCalendar. Thirty-four people showed up. Not bad.

A second way to spread the word about your event is to introduce a Twitter #hashtag and encourage people to use it leading up to the event. A #hashtag is simply a convention on Twitter where you precede a word with the "#" symbol, making it easier to search for. Twitter also makes #hashtags clickable, further supporting the search function. You can select any #hashtag you like. The #hashtag for the big South by Southwest conference in Austin is #sxsw. Some conferences include the year in their #hashtag so #sxsw could also be #sxsw2012. Anyway, once introduced, encourage people to include the #hashtag in their tweets.

At the end of every week or two, publish the "top tweets" as a blog post, giving credit to all the individual contributors. Simply gather all the tweets that included the conference #hashtag and pick the best ones. People love to be recognized for their tweets, particularly if it's on a website other than Twitter! Once published, you can use the same #hashtag to announce the blog post back on Twitter. You can also send @replies directly to the actual contributors, letting them know they were featured in your blog post. They'll appreciate it and will most likely retweet (RT) it to their own audiences. You're rewarding their engagement and that encourages more.

Go a step further and announce your new "top tweets" blog post as a new discussion within relevant Facebook and LinkedIn groups. Use the title "top 20 tweets about the upcoming #sxsw conference" to stir people's curiosity. What are the top 20 tweets? Who wrote them? This is a great way to drive traffic back to your blog and build buzz about the conference.

Next up: request photos of all your speakers. Pull them into Photoshop and brand them with the conference information, then upload them to your Facebook page. Tag the speaker featured in each photo (see Chapter 73 for instructions). Doing so will put these images (effectively advertisements for the conference) into their respective profiles and will also publish them on their respective walls. You have to be "friends" on Facebook before you can tag these speakers in photos. That means you'll have to send friend requests to your speakers before tagging them in photos, but that should be easy to do. Most speakers are pretty liberal with friend requests.

The best part is that the speakers appreciate the conference acknowledging their contribution with these images. In other words, you're not annoying anyone by doing this. Everyone likes it . . . and it drives registration! If you're curious to see an example of such images, Google "patrick schwerdtfeger" (include the quotation marks) and then click "images" on the left-hand sidebar. You'll find a bunch of images I created for myself. They're also on my Facebook page. In each case, I got an image of the city where I was scheduled to speak and then added my own head shot in the corner, along with the conference information. They look great and raise my profile as a speaker.

Invite your conference speakers to offer free bonuses to registrants. Perhaps it could be an educational e-book or a password-protected training video. In terms of registrations, bonuses are generally more effective than discounts. The speakers benefit by getting the e-mail addresses from those who claim their bonuses. Also, by adding up the "regular prices" of all these bonuses, you can legitimately advertise a huge value for the conference registration fee. (By the way, this fits perfectly into the beginner, intermediate, and advanced content framework we introduced in Chapters 22, 23, and 24.)

Ask your speakers to create short (one- or two-minute) videos of themselves talking about the upcoming conference. Perhaps they can talk about the bonus they're offering and why it's so valuable. Ideally, get a video from the conference hotel as well, showing the facilities where the conference will take place. You can then post those videos on Facebook and LinkedIn, and embed them on your blog, building even more excitement for the conference.

The objective is to get influencers talking about your conference or event. There are two categories of influencers: socially influential attendees and your speakers. Each one of these strategies targets one or the other. By giving them something to talk about, you're encouraging their engagement and leveraging their networks to accumulate registrations. Think about how you can use these strategies in your own business.

Implementation Checklist

- [ ] Visit the FullCalendar.com website.
- [ ] See if their service supports your city.
- [ ] If so, test it on your next event.
- [ ] Introduce a #hashtag for your event.
- [ ] Encourage people to use the #hashtag.
- [ ] Publish the "top tweets" on your blog.
- [ ] Notify everyone included via @replies.
- [ ] Publicize it in related groups as well.
- [ ] Get photos from all your speakers.
- [ ] Brand the photos with event details.
- [ ] Upload to Facebook and tag speakers.
- [ ] Invite speakers to offer bonuses.
- [ ] Promote the bonuses in announcements.
- [ ] Invite speakers to make short videos.
- [ ] Request a video from the hotel as well.
- [ ] Post these videos on your blog.
- [ ] Post them on Facebook and LinkedIn too.
- [ ] Compare notes and ideas with a colleague.

Chapter 60

Product Launch Formula

What's your limited time offer?

People respond to limited time offers. It fuels the sales process. If you're trying to sell something, you're generally better off offering some sort of discount, but only for a limited time. Or maybe the entire offering is only available for a limited time. Either way, limited time offers work.

You may already be familiar with Jeff Walker and his Product Launch Formula. Jeff has pioneered this approach online and has made millions in the process. For those of you who want to learn more, I recommend you search for "jeff walker product launch formula" and get on his e-mail list. The guy really knows his stuff. For now, let's look at the basics. Think back to Chapter 20, "Expand the Frame." Think back to the offering you considered in that chapter. Super high end, super expensive. Remember? The product launch strategy is a perfect way to "launch" an offering like that. According to Jeff Walker's Product Launch Formula, you might use the following format to promote the launch.

First, we need to incorporate video. It's way more effective than the other options. Next, we need it to be a limited time offer. We also need the launch to involve a sequence of events with a defined starting point and a defined ending point. The idea is to make your marketing an "event" rather than an ongoing campaign. Here's the basic formula:

On day one, you release the first of four videos. We're talking about a meaty 45-minute video with tons of value. Content, content, content. Help people. And the website where the video is displayed should be extremely clean with almost nothing else visible—just the video and a few tabs. The tabs should include Video 1, Video 2, Video 3, and Video 4 across the top (or down the side) but all the tabs except Video 1 should be shaded out for now.

And in Video 1, you should tell viewers that this is the first in a series of four free videos designed to deliver huge value and set you apart from anyone else in your field. Make sure the website allows comments and ask your viewers to post comments below the video. Tell them that their comments will be addressed in later videos. Even better, install the Facebook Comments Plugin so the comments get published on their Facebook profiles as well.

At the end of Video 1, tell your viewers that they need to enter their e-mail address to receive notification of the next three videos. Without entering their e-mail address, they won't receive the rest of the free content. So anyone can watch the first video. It's open. No firewall. Visitors can watch it without entering any information. But the next three videos require an e-mail address to access. Already at this point, the quality of your video is key. If the quality of the content is low, nobody will subscribe to receive the next three videos. So make it good! Give away some great content.

On day four, you send an e-mail to those who subscribed, informing them that Video 2 is now available and providing a link. The page with the video should now have the Video 1 and Video 2 tabs showing and the tabs for Video 3 and Video 4 still shaded out. Also, be sure to set your website such that people who have not subscribed are restricted from watching, unless they enter their e-mail address at that point. This type of website configuration requires some coding. The videos have to stream from somewhere (either your own server or a third-party provider such as Amazon Web Services) and the subscription firewalls mentioned above can be tricky. I've gone through this process myself and hired a web developer to put it all together. Unless you love coding, I recommend you do the same.

Video 2 offers even more content, another 30- to 45-minute video. Really try to offer killer content. You're trying to demonstrate your expertise and how much value you can bring to their businesses and their lives. Near the end of Video 2, tell your viewers that you'll be launching an amazing package deal (or bundle or whatever) at the end of the four-video series. Don't say much about it. Just make the announcement.

On day seven, send out an e-mail to your subscribers informing them that Video 3 is now available along with a link. On this page, the only tab left shaded out is Video 4. Video 3 is the bridge. It's where you switch over from valuable free content to promotion. Spend the first 20 minutes or so addressing things people wrote in the comments section of the first two videos. Spend the last 20 minutes telling them about all the information you have not yet shared—information that will be included in your package. Tell them how that information can change their businesses or even their lives. By the way, you don't have to wait for comments to come in from your first two videos before you record your third video. You can probably anticipate the questions people will have about your content and record the third video based on those expectations. Let them know that the package will become available on day 10 and that Video 4 will explain exactly what's included. On day 10, send an e-mail informing everyone that the final video and the package are now available. All four tabs are now fully visible.

Video 4 is all about describing the package you're selling. You need to tell them exactly what they'll be getting—the modules, the worksheets, the support resources, and the community. Tell them the price and that the package will only be available for three days. Send e-mails each day during that time and close the shopping cart at the scheduled time.

Following a sequence like this builds a lot of anticipation and can dramatically increase the price you're able to charge for your product or service. Also, if you package it right, this process can work for almost any type of business. I've heard of people using it to promote salsa dancing classes, guitar lessons, dog-training videos, and a three-day yoga retreat. All of the top Internet marketers are using this format to promote their products and services these days. Get creative. Think outside the box. I'm willing to bet there's a way for you to incorporate this strategy into your own business too.

Implementation Checklist

- ☐ Create an expensive package to sell.
- ☐ Create four videos to support the launch.
- ☐ Build a website to deliver the videos.
- ☐ Day 1: release Video 1 to your entire list.
- ☐ Use Video 1 to provide valuable content.
- ☐ Require an e-mail to see the other videos.
- ☐ Day 4: release Video 2 to subscribers.
- ☐ Use Video 2 to provide more content.
- ☐ Day 7: release Video 3 to subscribers.
- ☐ Use Video 3 to answer questions.
- ☐ Day 10: release Video 4 to subscribers.
- ☐ Use Video 4 to explain the package.
- ☐ Open the shopping cart for three days.
- ☐ Send one reminder e-mail each day.
- ☐ Close the shopping cart on schedule.
- ☐ Compare notes and ideas with a colleague.

Chapter 61

Build Massive Credibility

Why should I listen to *you*?!?

Credibility sits at the heart of business success, particularly if you're a service professional or a subject matter expert where people rely on (and pay you for) your expertise. Luckily, modern technology has created tons of great opportunities to demonstrate your expertise and build credibility fast. This chapter focuses on two of my favorites.

Record Your Own CD

Recording and producing an informational CD product—or a series of informational CDs—is a great way to build credibility. It's easier than you might think and the production costs are shockingly low.

Keep in mind that you can download the free Audacity recording software, buy a decent microphone with a pop filter (refer back to Chapter 51 for more details), and you're ready to go.

A typical CD runs about 60 minutes. Personally, I speak at a rate of about 140 words per minute. That means a CD represents about 8,400 words for me. In a standard Word document, that's about 17 typed pages. If you have an outline, you could probably write the whole text over a weekend.

Here's another approach. You can have a friend do an interview with you and record the whole thing. You could write a bunch of questions and prepare all your answers ahead of time. If you take this approach, you'll need a second microphone and a jack splitter to plug into your laptop. Otherwise, you could use FreeConferenceCall.com to make the recording.

In 2007, I produced 11 educational CD products and still sell a few of them on Amazon. They're produced by Kunaki.com in New York State. The customer service is pretty weak but you can't beat the prices. The CDs cost just $1.75 each (including the jewel case, UPC barcode, cellophane wrapping, and full color printing) and they have absolutely no minimums.

Did you catch that? No minimums! That means you can order *one* CD and it will cost you less than $2 plus shipping.

Kunaki also makes it easy to sell your CDs on Amazon and other online retail platforms. When I get reorder Purchase Orders from Amazon, I place the order with Kunaki and they ship directly to the Amazon distribution center in Lexington, Kentucky.

Amazon ranks high on Google. Anyone searching for me on Google will see that I have educational CDs available on Amazon and that positions me as an established authority in my field.

Before I published my first book, I used to bring those CDs to my speaking engagements. Again, it gave me added credibility and positioned me as an expert.

Record Your Own DVD

You can also create your own educational DVDs. Guess what they cost. You guessed it—$1.75 each with no minimums. That's right! Kunaki.com does both CDs and DVDs and the price is the same. As with CDs, the price includes a DVD case, UPC barcode, cellophane wrapping, and full color printing. It's truly an incredible deal.

DVDs have a higher perceived value than CDs, especially when packaged together as a set. For example, if you sold an individual DVD, an average price might range from $15 to $30. On the other hand, I created a six-DVD set in 2009 and sold it along with a workbook for $297. That's almost $50 per DVD and the value seemed perfectly reasonable.

Of course, recording a DVD is a bit more complicated than recording a CD. You need a 60-minute video. But yet again, there are strategies that make the process a lot less intimidating. The easiest way to create a 60-minute video (especially if you don't feel comfortable on video) is to use "screen capture" video recording software to record a PowerPoint presentation (or Keynote presentation if you're using a Mac) along with your voice narrating the slides.

Screen capture refers to software that captures whatever is on your computer screen. So if you had a PowerPoint presentation and ran through the slides, you could record it using screen capture software. You could also plug in a microphone and narrate each slide as you get to it. That means viewers would see the slides and hear your voice, but would never actually see you.

There are a number of advantages to this format approach. You don't need to create a studio environment. You don't need fancy lighting or an expensive camcorder. You don't need to memorize the entire presentation. You don't even need to take a shower! Nobody will see you anyway. The only thing you need to worry about is creating beautiful and informative slides, and narrating them with valuable content.

The leading screen capture video recording software is called Camtasia, created by TechSmith. At the time of this writing, it costs $299 and can be purchased directly on their website.

www.techsmith.com

Camtasia can also be used to edit traditional video footage recorded on other devices. Not only can you clip and rearrange video segments but you can add overlays, callouts, and special cursor effects. But *yes*, it does cost some money. If $299 is over your budget, there's an open source (meaning free—see Chapter 26) alternative called CamStudio. It's not nearly as powerful as Camtasia but you can download it free of charge.

http://camstudio.org

Of course, you can record an actual video featuring you in person. I'm only mentioning the above options because many people feel uncomfortable on video and use that as an excuse to avoid the project. Creating a DVD product doesn't have to be that difficult. You might even have a PowerPoint presentation that you've given in the past. If so, you could install the software and record your first DVD tonight!

Creating your own educational CDs and DVDs adds tremendous credibility to your business brand, even if you never sell a single copy. Yes, you can make good money selling educational products, but that's not the primary benefit. Build your credibility. Build your reputation. Build your brand.

Implementation Checklist

- ☐ Visit Kunaki.com and see their capabilities.
- ☐ Search for other CD production providers.
- ☐ Think about creating your own CD product.
- ☐ Write out the text or do an interview.
- ☐ Record the audio and upload to Kunaki.
- ☐ Sell your new CD product on Amazon.
- ☐ Consider creating your own DVD product.
- ☐ Build PowerPoint slides you could present.
- ☐ Practice running through your presentation.
- ☐ Learn about Camtasia at TechSmith.com.
- ☐ Learn about CamStudio at CamStudio.org.
- ☐ Pick one and record your presentation.
- ☐ Upload to Kunaki along with graphics.
- ☐ Sell your new DVD product on Amazon.
- ☐ Compare notes and ideas with a colleague.

Part Six

Leverage Social Media

Chapter 62

Social Media Mantras

Content is *King* . . . or is it?

This is a very common phrase on the Internet. And in years gone by, it was very true. The single most important ingredient for online success was good-quality content. Today, with the social media revolution in full effect, I no longer agree with that statement. To me . . .

Content is . . . *Queen.*

When the first version of my book launched, one reader was quite offended by this analogy. She argued it was sexist. So let me be clear: in no way am I making any inference about the sexes or which deserves to be on top. As far as I'm concerned, men and women are equally valuable in our society.

The point is that "content is king" implies that content is the single most important ingredient. That's no longer true. So what took its place? What's now in the top spot?

Community Engagement

Community engagement is *King*. There is a very clear reason why this is true. Here goes. Bad-quality content combined with community engagement beats good-quality content by itself.

Bad Content + Community Engagement > Good Content

Now, if you have good-quality content *and* community engagement, you win. No question. But even bad-quality content can find an audience with effective community engagement. So what is community engagement? It's your participation in the conversation (see Chapter 44). It's what we've been talking about throughout this book. When you make a contribution to your community without trying to sell a product, you're engaging your community. You're participating in the conversation. Community engagement is the essence of the modern Internet. Community engagement is at the center of the social media revolution. Conversations are markets. Embrace this mantra and your journey on the Internet will be far more productive. So, community engagement is *King*. Content is *Queen*. What's in third place?

Authenticity and Transparency

Authenticity and transparency are critical on the Internet. For better or for worse, the days of secrets are behind us. As soon as you try to put a spin on something, your audience will drop you like a rock. If you're caught in a lie, you're finished. The best thing you can do today is freely admit your weaknesses and your failures. People are people. We all have shortcomings. Strive to be flawed. Perfection is passé. What do you think when you see a perfectly produced video? You probably assume it was done by a professional marketing company. And as enjoyable as it might be to watch, you probably trust it less than an amateur-looking alternative of a real person with a real message. Authenticity makes you a person, not a business. And transparency adds credibility to your message. Adopt these mantras and your actions will speak to the masses. Ignore them and your message will fall flat.

Implementation Checklist

- [ ] Community engagement is *King*.
- [ ] Good-quality content is *Queen*.
- [ ] Authenticity and transparency comes in third.
- [ ] Participate in the conversation.
- [ ] Always provide value to your audience.
- [ ] Be a person first and a business second.
- [ ] Compare notes and ideas with a colleague.

Chapter 63

Social Media Integration

Are you too busy?

It's usually about this time that people start throwing their hands in the air. If you started at the beginning of this book, you've gone through 62 chapters so far. We've discussed a lot of different things. How are you supposed to do all these new activities when you're far too busy already?!

Fear not.

Indeed, there are lots of platforms that all represent opportunities for you to build credibility and gain exposure online, but that doesn't mean you need to spend hours on each one. Turns out, one of the biggest trends of our day is integration. Many of these social media platforms integrate easily with each other. And once integrated, your activity on one is automatically announced on the others. That means you could do something on one platform and have four or five different audiences (or more) notified all at the same time!

This stems from the primary difference between blogs and websites that we introduced first in Chapter 27. You can *subscribe* to a blog. You can't subscribe to a website. Blogs have what's called an RSS feed. Well, so do all the other social media platforms! In that earlier chapter, we discussed how Facebook, LinkedIn, and Twitter can all subscribe to your blog. Well, they can all subscribe to each other too. Your Facebook profile has an RSS feed. So does your LinkedIn profile. They all do. So they can all be connected together.

Let me describe how I have my own accounts connected. Basically, I want everything I do online to eventually end up on my Twitter feed. If I post something on my blog, I want it announced on Twitter. If I upload a video on YouTube, I want it on Twitter. If I update my status on Facebook,

I want it on Twitter. The easiest way to do that is to route everything through FriendFeed.

Create a FriendFeed account at FriendFeed.com and click "settings" and then "add/edit" to configure everything. It connects with everything! Then select the "Twitter publishing preferences" to push everything (except tweets from Twitter) to Twitter. The result is that everything you do online ends up on Twitter. I also have my blog integrated with my Facebook and LinkedIn profiles, so my blog posts automatically populate Facebook and LinkedIn. I push my YouTube channel and Meetup group to Facebook as well. Hmmm. Anything else? Probably. Bottom line: I try to integrate everything I can.

The point of this chapter is to encourage you to leverage these platforms and to do so in the most efficient way possible. They're extremely powerful and don't cost anything to try. So what's the harm? Setting it all up takes a little time. But once that's done, your online presence is integrated.

Different people use the Internet in different ways. Some like blogs. Some like videos or photos. Some like audio recordings. And some just spend time on social networks. Find ways to tie them all together so your contributions are automatically distributed to each. Multiplatform integration is at the center of the buzz these days. You'll see more and more of this as time passes. Get started now so you can ride the wave that's driving the Internet into the future.

Implementation Checklist

- [ ] Create an account on FriendFeed.
- [ ] Integrate everything on FriendFeed.
- [ ] Push all your online activity to Twitter.
- [ ] Push your blog to Facebook and LinkedIn.
- [ ] Push YouTube to your Facebook profile.
- [ ] Push Meetup to your Facebook profile.
- [ ] Always look for more integration features.
- [ ] Compare notes and ideas with a colleague.

Chapter 64

Twitter
Share Tips

Is Twitter a complete waste of time?

Many people think so. And for those who do, they'll love this study done by Pear Analytics in 2009. After monitoring hundreds of thousands of tweets, the researchers categorized a full 40 percent as "pointless babble." The people who hate Twitter look at this study and use it to justify why they don't want to be on Twitter. I look at the same study and see it as precisely the reason why I do want to be on Twitter. Most people on Twitter are sharing completely useless updates like, "I'm going to get a taco." Who cares about the taco?! The same study concluded that just 8.7 percent of tweets had what they refer to as "pass-along value." Less than 10 percent were good enough that people shared them with their friends. It's not hard to shine in this audience! It's a fairly low bar.

Very few people are actually providing value on Twitter and that's precisely where the opportunity lies. When I launched the first version of this book in March 2009, I summarized it into 300 marketing tips and then released those tips as tweets on Twitter. Each tip offered some tiny piece of advice. One read "Conversations are markets. Participation + Facilitation = Opportunity. More tips at www.WebifyBook.com."

What was I doing? I was trying to introduce myself on the raging river called Twitter . . . and if people reading my tip weren't interested, that's okay. But if they got some value from it, they could click through to my website and learn more about me. Write a list of 200 or 300 tips. You already have the expertise. Over the course of a weekend, just about anyone could put together a list of useful tips. Then release those tips on Twitter and start providing value.

I uploaded all my tips to an automated platform called TweetLater.com, later renamed SocialOomph.com. I scheduled the tips to go out once each day for 300 days. I also uploaded a series of inspiring quotes and had them go out once each day as well. That means the "value" portion of my Twitter contributions went out whether I was logged into the platform or not.

www.socialoomph.com

By the way, when I first started, I actually scheduled the tips to go out once each hour, 16 times each day. Big mistake. It was way too much. People got annoyed. So over time, I reduced it to eight per day, then four per day, and finally down to just one each day. Do whatever you like but keep in mind that dumping a ton of automated tweets onto Twitter is quickly recognized and people don't like it.

Another mistake: I initially pushed all of my tweets to my Facebook profile. Bad idea. The culture on Facebook is different. Most people don't update their status on Facebook multiple times each day. Also, the vernacular on Twitter is distinctive and my Facebook friends immediately recognized that my status updates originated on Twitter. Again, do what you like but I recommend making separate contributions on Facebook. In fact, pushing your Facebook updates to Twitter (instead of the other way around) works much better. So my Facebook updates end up on Twitter (via FriendFeed) but my tweets do *not* end up on Facebook. (See Chapter 63 for more details on this.)

There are four reasons to tweet.

1. *Wisdom:* Demonstrate your expertise. My marketing tips were a perfect example. Show your knowledge. Provide value. That's the stuff people end up passing along to their friends.
2. *Business:* Tell people about your products or services. Don't overdo it; maybe one out of every ten tweets. But it's okay to tell your followers what you do.
3. *Life:* Share a little bit of your personal life. Believe it or not, some people like the tweets about getting a taco. They want to interact with a human being, not just a business.
4. *Community:* Interact with your community. Reply to other people's tweets. Retweet (RT) good ones to your own followers. Participate in the conversation. It's fun and will benefit your business.

Implementation Checklist

☐ Write a list of 200 or 300 helpful tips.
☐ Visit the SocialOomph.com website.
☐ Consider signing up for an account.
☐ Don't publish too many automated tweets.
☐ Avoid pushing your tweets to Facebook.
☐ Instead, push Facebook updates to Twitter.
☐ Wisdom: share insights with followers.
☐ Business: tell followers what you sell.
☐ Life: share some personal details as well.
☐ Community: interact with your followers.
☐ Compare notes and ideas with a colleague.

Chapter 65

Twitter
Search Keywords

Are you finding new customers on Twitter?

There are lots of great Twitter success stories but one of my favorites involves JetBlue Airways. They have people on staff who search Twitter for people who are tweeting the word "Southwest." In particular, they search for people who are saying not-so-nice things about their competitors. And what does it give them the opportunity to do? They can reply—in real time—to people who need their services at the *precise* moment they might be unhappy with the competition.

That's borderline "evil" . . . but it's brilliant too.

I worked with a lady who has a small flower store. Actually, it isn't even a real store. It's a kiosk with wheels on the bottom, so she wheels it out every morning and sells flowers to people walking past. We accumulated a local following for her on Twitter (using Twellow.com) and she checks her feed every morning to look for people in her following who tweeted the words "baby," "wedding," "congratulations" and a half a dozen other words. And where appropriate, she replies with:

@username Saw your tweet. Congratulations from us as well. Come on in and get a free flower. [link to Yelp profile]

Most people don't take her up on the offer. But some do and more than half buy something when they're there! Get it? This lady is using the "waste of time" Twitter to find new customers every day. What words could you search for? Go to:

http://search.twitter.com

Play with it. Search for your favorite keywords and see what you find. Think about phrases your ideal customers might be using in their tweets and then search for those phrases. You might be surprised at what you find. Searching for an appropriate phrase is important. If you search for just your primary keywords, you'll find all your competitors. Instead, think of a phrase your ideal customer might use in a conversation with friends, and search for that. I recently spoke at a conference of insurance agents and did some research leading up to the event. I searched for "I need new insurance" and immediately found people who were looking for suggestions on insurance providers. Actually, I was surprised how many applicable tweets I found.

Keep in mind that you can reply to *anyone* on Twitter, whether you're following them or they're following you or not. For the people looking for insurance advice, an insurance agent could reply with:

@username Saw your tweet about insurance. That's what we do! Here's a free PDF report with some answers http://bit.ly/insurance-advice.

By including the @username format, the recipient will get notified about your tweet, even if he or she has never heard of you before. The report is important as well. Step 1 for Internet marketing: create a juicy sexy PDF report you can give away for free. It's not a sales pitch. It's a valuable report designed to help your customers and prospects. It could be your intermediate content from Chapter 23. It's a lot easier to introduce yourself to strangers by giving them something for free first, rather than assaulting them with a blatant sales pitch. Obviously, you can include a call to action inside the report that talks about your business but the overwhelming purpose is to provide value. You can use a report like that in a million different ways. The insurance tweet above is just one example. So make sure you have a value-packed report available. You'll be happy you did.

Now go ahead and visit search.twitter.com and search for some keywords and phrases. If the results don't seem relevant, that's fine. Just test it. It might put some ideal prospects right in front of your nose.

Implementation Checklist

- ☐ Visit the search.twitter.com website.
- ☐ Search for relevant keywords in your field.
- ☐ Search for phrases prospects might use.
- ☐ Create a value-packed PDF report.
- ☐ Include a call to action inside the report.
- ☐ Reply to applicable tweets, offering help.
- ☐ Include a link to the value-packed PDF.
- ☐ Monitor reaction and adjust if necessary.
- ☐ Compare notes and ideas with a colleague.

Chapter 66

Twitter

Incentivize Interaction

Do your customers tell their friends about you?

There's a company in New Orleans that's using Twitter in a very interesting way. The company is called Naked Pizza (great name!) and they embraced Twitter by putting a large sign in front of their retail location, encouraging people to follow them on Twitter. Naked Pizza has used social media extensively and has become a poster child for modern online marketing. What if they offered a 10 percent discount to people who *tweeted* their orders in? Consider the implications. Why would people do it? The discount? Perhaps, but there's more . . .

I have more than 25,000 followers on Twitter. If I tweeted my order in, everyone in my network would be notified that I just ordered pizza from Naked Pizza. The "viral" element is baked in! It's guaranteed.

How can you incentivize your *existing* customers to communicate with you through the social channel? Right now, they call you on the phone. That's private. They e-mail you. That's private. But if they interact with you on Twitter, their networks are notified. If they interact with you on Facebook, their networks are notified. By tweeting my pizza order in, I am automatically telling my entire network that I order my pizza from Naked Pizza! It's a winning strategy. The most important part is the incentive being offered. Social media success is driven by incentives. Make it worthwhile and keep in mind that the discount will replace what you would've otherwise spent on traditional marketing. Giving that money back to the customer through social media like Twitter has far more potential than giving it to an advertising salesperson!

Everyone wants to know the return on investment (ROI) of social media. It's a very difficult question to answer. Social media (such as Twitter) is a communication channel. What's the ROI of a communication channel? It's like asking what the ROI is of your cell phohe. It's really hard to measure.

It's much easier to measure the ROI of a marketing campaign that offers an incentive and runs *through* a communication channel. That works. Incentives are an essential ingredient in social media marketing. Offer a discount or a free gift, even if it's small. Doing so will allow you to measure exactly how many people took advantage of the offer. It allows you to measure the ROI.

Incorporate incentives in everything you do on social media platforms. Make a list of all the little incentives you could offer and start testing them. Try different things and measure the response to each one. It won't take long and you'll start to understand precisely what motivates your audience—what drives them to take action. Once you understand that equation, your marketing gets a lot easier.

Think about how you might use incentives in your business. Perhaps you can have a contest. Maybe you can offer an incentive just like the one I suggest for Naked Pizza. Whatever you decide, it's a powerful way to get your customers to spread the word about you and your products or services.

Implementation Checklist

- ☐ Consider existing customer interactions.
- ☐ Can you move them to social channels?
- ☐ Make a list of incentives you could offer.
- ☐ Offer an incentive to interact via Twitter.
- ☐ Hold a contest with interaction on Twitter.
- ☐ Make sure the incentive is worthwhile.
- ☐ Monitor results and adjust if necessary.
- ☐ Compare notes and ideas with a colleague.

Chapter 67

LinkedIn
Precision E-mails

Do you get more than 50 e-mails each day?

For most, the answer is *yes*. You might even get more than 100 each day. By contrast, how many LinkedIn e-mails do you get each day? Five? Ten? For savvy LinkedIn users, maybe more but it's still a small number compared to your regular e-mail. Turns out, e-mails that come through LinkedIn get opened a lot more than regular e-mails. These are the types of statistics LinkedIn publicizes on their blog because they demonstrate the value of the LinkedIn platform.

Consider unsolicited e-mails, e-mails from people you don't know. So we're not talking about e-mails from your spouse, colleagues, or friends. If you get an unsolicited e-mail, you're up to seven times as likely to open that e-mail if it came through LinkedIn rather than if it just showed up in your regular e-mail inbox. LinkedIn is a great way to deliver a proposal to an ideal prospect, especially for people in the B2B (business to business) space. You have a much better chance that the prospect will actually open your e-mail and see what you have to say.

If you're a savvy LinkedIn user, you'll know that you can only send LinkedIn e-mails—called "InMail"—to your direct network, people you're directly connected to. As luck would have it, there's a really easy way around that. Just visit the profile of the person you're trying to contact—all LinkedIn profiles are public so you can visit anyone's profile—and see which groups he or she is a member of. Join one of the same groups and once approved, you can send InMail to anyone in a mutual group. This is not always true. There are settings people can modify in their group membership preferences and it is possible for people to restrict the messages they get from other group members. But the default setting allows other group members to be able to send them InMail directly, and most people leave those default settings unchanged.

Here's what most people do: they join groups full of their competitors. It makes perfect sense. So a photographer joins groups of photographers. And that's fine. I'm not suggesting you stop doing that. Rather, I'm suggesting you go a step further. Take a moment and think about what groups your customers and prospects would be a part of. Visit the Groups tab on LinkedIn and do some searches to see what you can find. Visit the LinkedIn profiles of your best customers. See what groups they're a member of. Select a few groups—ideally, the big ones—and join. It'll give you direct access to your ideal prospects.

For me, I'm always connecting with event planners. Those are the people who hire speakers. On LinkedIn, there are some huge groups of event planners, including Event Peeps and Meeting Professionals International (MPI). I joined both of those groups and it's a tremendous marketing channel for me. The Meeting Professionals International (MPI) group has more than 18,000 members. It's a raging river all on its own. It's an online destination with tons of traffic, all of whom are ideal prospects for me. By being a member of that group, I have direct access to my target market.

How would you contact these prospects? This may seem obvious but you'd be surprised how few people do it correctly. If you're about to send a message to someone you don't know, take a few minutes and visit the person's LinkedIn profile first. Look for commonalities you can mention in your message to make it less "cold" and more personal. Upon visiting the person's profile, perhaps you'll notice that you went to the same alma mater. You'll see if you have any mutual contacts. And obviously, you'll know the group you're both a member of. Include those specifics in your message. "I'm contacting you to introduce myself. We're both members of [group name] and I noticed we have two mutual contacts: Chris and Lisa. I also saw that you went to Cal. Me too! Anyway, I believe we might be able to help each other." And so on.

The point is your message should be as personal and relevant as possible. If it's not, the recipient might tag your message as spam and that can result in your account being frozen, suspended, or even deleted. I am absolutely *not* suggesting you send spammy e-mails to people you find on LinkedIn. Instead, take the time to research the person you're about to contact and then introduce yourself in the most relevant way possible. It's a discipline, just like going to the gym. I've used this analogy before but it's true here too. Go in January and the place is packed. Go in March and it's empty. That's the reality. Similarly, we all know the right things to eat but rarely eat the right things! Most people don't take the extra five or ten minutes to customize their e-mails, but that extra effort makes all the difference in the world. There are highly successful salespeople who use nothing but LinkedIn to facilitate their sales efforts. You could be doing that too.

Implementation Checklist

- ☐ Visit the Groups tab on LinkedIn.
- ☐ Search for your keywords.
- ☐ Look for groups full of prospects.
- ☐ Avoid groups full of your competitors.
- ☐ Visit some customer profiles on LinkedIn.
- ☐ See what groups they're a member of.
- ☐ Join some of the same groups.
- ☐ Visit profiles before sending messages.
- ☐ Look for commonalities you can mention.
- ☐ Contact prospects by providing value first.
- ☐ Be as personal and relevant as possible.
- ☐ Compare notes and ideas with a colleague.

Chapter 68

LinkedIn

Profile Basics

Is your LinkedIn profile complete?

For most, the answer is *yes* . . . *but* . . . You may have filled out your profile. You may have answered all the questions. You may have even included all the correct dates and locations and job descriptions. But chances are you're missing a few important opportunities. Let's look at a few.

Status Updates

Did you know you can update your status on LinkedIn? It's true. You can update your status whenever you like, just like you can on Facebook. And of course, Twitter focuses exclusively on status updates. Anyway, you can update your status on LinkedIn too. The important thing is where that update goes. It gets displayed right at the top of your profile, immediately below your name and photo. That's some valuable real estate! I'm willing to bet that anyone visiting your profile will see your status update. It's a great place for an announcement. There's an endless list of things you can mention in your status update but I recommend something pointing to an informative video or that juicy sexy PDF report we talked about in Chapter 65. The beauty is that you can include a live link, allowing people to click through.

"Here's a 5-minute video with the seven biggest mistakes people make when renovating their kitchen: [link to YouTube video]"

"Here's a free 14-page PDF report with the 25 most effective promotional products of 2010: [link to PDF report]"

Whatever you point to, take advantage of that real estate and get something up there. Also, keep in mind that your status update is included in the weekly e-mail LinkedIn users get with "updates from people you know." That means it makes sense to update your status once each week but not necessarily more than that.

Recommendations

Do you have any recommendations on LinkedIn? You should: people read them! So whether you like LinkedIn recommendations or not, it makes sense to get a few. What's the easiest way to get them? Well, you could simply request them, but I find that a bit tacky. Or you could sit back and pray that people you know will write them proactively. Good luck with that. Or . . . Think back to that great client you had 18 months ago. Boy, wouldn't your life be easier right now if you had that client again! Have you written a recommendation for that person? Perhaps. But for most, the answer is *no,* even though you loved working with that person and have nothing but good things to say about him or her. What would happen if you wrote that recommendation today? Well, he or she (let's say it's a she) would get an e-mail saying that you just wrote a recommendation for her on LinkedIn. She would immediately be reminded of you and how nice it was to work with you—objective 1 accomplished. Next, she would read the recommendation and it would presumably include some complimentary comments. Pretty cool. I suspect she would sincerely appreciate the gesture—objective 2 accomplished. At the bottom of the e-mail, she would have the option to either accept the recommendation or ignore it. What would happen if she clicks "Accept"? LinkedIn would take her to precisely the spot on their platform where she can return the favor! It would literally say "The recommendation has been posted to your profile. Why not return the favor and recommend [your name] back."

Take a Saturday afternoon and write a dozen recommendations for people you're connected to on LinkedIn and for whom you have genuinely good things to say. Scroll through your LinkedIn contacts. If you have something nice to say, say it! By doing so, you'll tickle all those people's memories and more than likely get a bunch of recommendations back.

Website Links

You can include up to three links on your LinkedIn profile but the labels are very generic and boring: my blog, my website, and my company. You can customize those labels and it only takes about two minutes. Click "Edit My Profile" to change them. I use:

"Book me for your next event"—points to my "speaking" website.

"Marketing Shortcuts: my book"—points to my "book" website.

"Read a Sample Chapter (PDF)"—points to a PDF sample chapter.

The idea is to entice the reader and offer more visibility to where these links point to. Customizing your LinkedIn profile links gives people a better reason to make that click to find out more about you.

Implementation Checklist

- ☐ Update your status on LinkedIn.
- ☐ Include a link to something valuable.
- ☐ Consider updating your status weekly.
- ☐ Write recommendations for people.
- ☐ If you have something nice to say, say it!
- ☐ Customize the three links on your profile.
- ☐ Again, point those links to things of value.
- ☐ Tell the reader where the link points to.
- ☐ Compare notes and ideas with a colleague.

Chapter 69

LinkedIn

Google Ranking

Does your LinkedIn profile rank high on Google?

Chances are, if you Google your own name, your LinkedIn profile will show up on the first page. Of course, if you have a very common name, that won't be the case. You might have to include a few more keywords that identify what you do for business. But either way, LinkedIn profiles generally rank high on Google. Why is that? Is it because LinkedIn ranks well for people's names? Or is it because LinkedIn ranks high in general? The answer is that LinkedIn ranks high in general. It ranks for your name but it also ranks for all the other keywords that are listed in your profile.

Your LinkedIn profile has a "Summary" section at the top, including a "Specialties" heading. You also have a section under each job where you can discuss the particulars of that employment situation. Those are all great places to add specific keywords. LinkedIn has much more profile information than most of the other social media platforms. Consider Twitter, Facebook, and YouTube. None of them have anywhere close to the detailed personal information available on LinkedIn. Because LinkedIn is basically an online resume, it contains an enormous amount of personal information about its users. By the way, one of the most powerful characteristics of LinkedIn is that you can search by job title. You can't do that on Facebook or Twitter. You can't do that on YouTube. Yes, there are ways of identifying your target market on those other platforms, but LinkedIn actually has a formal way of searching by job title. That's one of the primary reasons why it's such a great marketing tool.

The point is that you can put a lot of information into your LinkedIn profile and you should strive to include as many keywords as you can. The trick? Be specific! Obviously, the generic keywords like "real estate" or "mortgage" or "coach" or "consultant" are highly competitive on Google so there's little sense in targeting them. But the specific and technical terms are a different story.

Recently, I spoke at an event held by the Bay Area Biomedical Consultants Network (BABCN). In preparation for that event, I did some general research about the biomedical field (to make my presentation more relevant to attendees) and found dozens of highly specialized terms specific to that industry. Including these types of specific keywords in your LinkedIn profile makes it distinctly possible you'll rank high on Google when people search for those words, particularly if they include a location name in their search query. Regardless of what you do for a living, try to identify the most specific terms possible, not because everybody is searching for those technical terms but because they're the easiest to rank for.

What we're trying to do is get you "found" on Google when people are searching for the specific things you do. Resist the urge to use the common generic terms in your industry. You'll never rank for those terms on a LinkedIn profile. They're just too competitive. And keep in mind that those who search for super specific and technical terms on Google are much better qualified prospects. They're demonstrating their knowledge of your industry by including those specific words. The more specific, the better.

If you are a service provider, it's likely your prospects include your location name when searching for your services. If they didn't, they might find a provider on the other side of the country or the other side of the world. So it makes sense to include the city, county, or state name in the search query. That means you should strive to include those words in your LinkedIn profile as well. Write down a list of location-based keywords including your city, neighboring cities, county, and state or province. If you're in a big city, perhaps you should even include the neighborhood keywords. Refer back to Chapter 13 to research which of these keywords are searched for the most on Google and then include the most commonly used search terms in your LinkedIn profile. Never miss an opportunity to add some keywords into your profile. You never know what quirky keyword phrase someone might use. Every time you add another keyword, you increase the odds that someone will find you.

Implementation Checklist

- ☐ List specific keywords in your industry.
- ☐ Include them in your "Summary" section.
- ☐ Include them in your "Specialties" section.
- ☐ Include them in your past job listings.
- ☐ Be specific, including technical terms.
- ☐ Make a list of location-based keywords.
- ☐ Use those in your profile as well.
- ☐ Consider what people might search for.
- ☐ Compare notes and ideas with a colleague.

Chapter 70

LinkedIn
Pimp Your Profile

Do you have a killer LinkedIn profile?

Turns out, there are tons of things you can do to spice it up. Here's the thing: people are visiting your profile whether you realize it or not. They're poking around, reading your stuff, and you almost never hear about their experience. So it makes sense to make your profile as impressive as you possibly can. The key to beefing up your profile lies in the "applications" available. On the top navigation bar, click "More" and then "Get more applications." There are many options; let's look at a few.

WordPress or Blog Link

These blog-related applications allow you to integrate your blog with your profile. By doing so, any blog posts you publish will automatically populate your LinkedIn profile at the same time. There are two applications relating to blogs: one for WordPress and one for all the others (Blog Link). So depending on which platform you're using, select the appropriate application and get it installed.

Amazon Bookshelf

If you've written a book, it makes good sense to use the Amazon Bookshelf application to highlight that book on your profile. Not only will it add credibility by showing the title you've published but it'll also include a link to

Amazon where people can buy your book. Incidentally, you can easily write a 20- or 30-page PDF document and sell it on Amazon for a few dollars. In other words, it doesn't need to be a full book. You can take a document you already have and set it up as a digital e-book for sale on Amazon. Once set up, you can then feature that product using the Amazon Bookshelf application—awesome credibility and it's not that hard. (Refer to Chapter 61 for more information on building other credibility products like CDs and DVDs.)

SlideShare

SlideShare is a platform where you can share PowerPoint presentations, PDF files, and other digital resources. It's becoming increasingly well known and attracts more and more users every day. LinkedIn offers a SlideShare application where you can include up to three files right on your LinkedIn profile. That means you can have a PowerPoint presentation or a detailed PDF proposal available right on LinkedIn. Take a moment to open a SlideShare account and upload a few files. Perhaps you have a PowerPoint presentation your prospects might benefit from. What about that juicy sexy PDF report we talked about in Chapter 65? Or maybe you have a proposal that's worth sharing. Adding these things to your LinkedIn profile allows visitors to learn more about you and your business (and your value proposition) right from their Internet browser.

TripIt

If you travel a lot (like I do), the TripIt application can add a lot of fun to your LinkedIn interactions. TripIt is a platform that tracks your trips and shares them in a social setting. You can follow other people's travels and they can follow yours. TripIt also integrates nicely with a variety of social media platforms including Facebook. Anyway, the TripIt application on LinkedIn will display your upcoming trips on your LinkedIn profile. Also, when you add a new trip, it will include it in the weekly e-mail all LinkedIn users receive with "updates from people you know." Every time I post a new trip on my TripIt account, it goes out to my LinkedIn network and I invariably get an e-mail or two from contacts who live in the destination city. As a result, I regularly have lunch with people in my network in cities all around the world.

Google Presentations

I have used the Google Presentations application to embed a video on my LinkedIn profile. This is a fun one; it's not as easy as some of the other ways you can dress up your profile, but it's worth the extra effort. At the time of this writing, LinkedIn has not provided an easy way to embed videos. But with the Google Presentations application, you can jerry-rig it to create that result. Here's what I did: I created a one-slide Google presentation and embedded a YouTube video on that slide. I then expanded the video window to encompass the entire slide and saved it with a privacy setting of "public." I then "shared" that presentation using the Google Presentations application on my LinkedIn profile. The result: I now have a YouTube video right on my profile. Of course, you can use this same application to include other presentations with multiple slides and graphics. Get creative. This is a great opportunity to put some impressive content on your LinkedIn profile.

Company Buzz or Tweets

LinkedIn also provides a way for you to include tweets on your profile. There are two applications serving that purpose and they allow you to do slightly different things. Company Buzz allows you to select certain searches (like your company name, for example) and have the applicable tweets show up on your LinkedIn profile. On the other hand, the Tweets application allows you to display your own most recent tweets on your profile. Essentially, Company Buzz allows you to display what *other people* are saying on Twitter while Tweets allows you to display what *you* are saying on Twitter. Tweets also allows you to follow, reply to, and retweet posts by people you're following, right from LinkedIn.

Other Applications

LinkedIn also provides an Events application. This one is great for finding events that people in your network are attending. If you're a lawyer, the Lawyer Ratings application might work well. If you're a real estate agent, Real Estate Pro will allow people in your network to follow your activities. And if you have certified SAP expertise, you can use SAP Community Bio to display those credentials on your LinkedIn profile.

Do you have to use all of these applications? Of course not. But they exist and you should play with each of them to see if you can use them. As we said at the beginning, people are already visiting your LinkedIn profile. Some probably visited while you were at home sleeping. You want those people to get the best impression possible, so take the time to beef up your LinkedIn profile. LinkedIn has ambitious plans to add new applications in the years ahead, so it makes sense to check back from time to time to see if anything new has been introduced. It's fun and will make you look like a technology ninja to all your connections!

Implementation Checklist

- ☐ Visit LinkedIn and click "More" at the top.
- ☐ Then click "Get more applications."
- ☐ Browse through the other applications.
- ☐ Look at the blog integration applications.
- ☐ Look at the Amazon Bookshelf.
- ☐ If you travel a lot, look at TripIt.
- ☐ Use Google Presentations to embed video.
- ☐ Check out Company Buzz and Tweets.
- ☐ Check back to see new options over time.
- ☐ Compare notes and ideas with a colleague.

Chapter 71

Facebook
Facilities

Can you use Facebook for business?

Yes! Absolutely. But we need to begin with some of the basics. There are three different "facilities" you can use on Facebook: profiles, groups, and pages. Profiles are for individuals. You probably already have a profile. Profiles have "friends." Groups are for multiple individuals with similar interests. Groups are built by profiles. A profile builds a group. Groups have "members." Pages are specifically designed for public figures and businesses. Pages are built by profiles. A profile builds and becomes an "admin" for a page. Pages have "fans" or "likes."

In the past, engaging with a page involved clicking a button called "become a fan," hence the term "fan." In 2010, Facebook replaced that vernacular with the "like" button. The change has resulted in an increased willingness of Facebook users to engage with Facebook pages. Anyway, both terms are regularly used to refer to page membership. Facebook pages can have multiple admins. You can add admins or remove them as circumstances change in your business. Also, when you become an admin for a page, it will not link back to your personal profile so it's a great way to keep your business and personal lives separate.

Now, let's take a look at how the Facebook facilities are different from each other.

If you want to see my profile, you have to jump over *two* hurdles to get there. First, you have to be on Facebook yourself. You have to have your own profile and be logged in. Second, you and I need to be Facebook "friends" for you to see my profile. There are a few exceptions to this.

Facebook recently introduced new privacy settings that allow you to make your profile more public. But for most people, there are two hurdles to viewing a profile.

If you want to see my group, there's only *one* hurdle you have to jump over. You have to have your own profile and be logged in, but you and I do not have to be friends for you to see my group. You can search for groups, find mine, and check it out without being friends with me.

If you want to see my page, there are *zero* hurdles. What does that mean? It means you don't even have to be logged in to Facebook to check out my page. It means there's no firewall. It means that pages are fully indexed by Google and the other search engines! Do you think Facebook ranks high on Google? Yes, indeed! Facebook is a huge website and Facebook pages rank high on Google. In fact, there are companies who have a Facebook page and a website, and when they search for their own company name on Google, their Facebook page ranks higher than their own website!

So that means there's an opportunity for businesses in creating Facebook pages for themselves. But wait! You need to keep one thing in mind: the title of your Facebook page is the only thing you can't change (once you have more than 100 fans). Everything else you can change, but not the title. So you want to get it right at the beginning.

The title of your Facebook page is the most valuable from a search engine optimization (SEO) perspective. For those familiar with the HTML website coding language, it's effectively your H1 tag. That's valuable real estate so you want to include some keywords if possible (and appropriate). If you work for a large company that people are already searching for, fine. Just use the company name for your page title. But if you're a self-employed service practitioner, you might want to include a few keywords beyond just your name. Would you call your page "Jane Smith?" No. Nobody is searching for "Jane Smith." Instead, call it "Jane Smith Financial Advisor Boston MA." There will be people searching for a financial advisor in Boston, so include those words in your page title.

Your Facebook page title is one of the only things you can't change. You can at the beginning but once you have more than 100 fans, the title will become permanent and will no longer be editable. If you already have more than 100 fans and are now wishing you could go back and change your page title—chill. It's not that big of a deal. It's just one of those little tricks that's worth mentioning for those who are just getting started. So if you have less than 100 fans, consider adding a few keywords. If you have more than 100 fans, it's probably not worth deleting it and building a new one. Stick with the one you have.

The important thing is to recognize the different facilities available on Facebook and how you can use them. Do not create a profile for your business. Profiles are for people, not businesses. Profiles that are created for businesses will eventually get deleted because they're against the Facebook terms of service. Create a *page* for your business. All the new features such as Facebook Places and Facebook Deals (Chapter 74) are only accessible through pages, leaving businesses with profiles in the cold.

Implementation Checklist

- ☐ Create a Facebook profile for yourself.
- ☐ Visit www.facebook.com/groups.
- ☐ Search for your favorite keywords.
- ☐ Visit www.facebook.com/pages.
- ☐ Search for your favorite keywords.
- ☐ Consider creating your own page.
- ☐ Never create a profile for a business.
- ☐ Add keywords to your page title.
- ☐ Compare notes and ideas with a colleague.

Chapter 72

Facebook

Communication

How do you communicate with your friends and fans?

This is another interesting topic on Facebook. Turns out, every facility you use (profiles, groups, or pages) has its own communication advantages. If I (my profile) want to send you (your profile) a message on Facebook, it will go into your Facebook inbox but you will also get e-mail notification (with the default settings). You'll get an e-mail telling you that Patrick (me) sent you a message on Facebook, and you can read the message in either location. To be clear, you can read my message in your regular e-mail inbox *or* you can log into Facebook and read my message in your Facebook inbox. The message is in both locations.

It gets interesting with groups and pages. If a group wants to send a message to its members, the delivery depends on the number of members in the group. If the group has 5,000 or fewer members, the message will go to each member's Facebook inbox *and* the group members will also get e-mail notification. If the group's membership grows to 5,001 members or more, the e-mail notification goes away. That means the message only goes to the Facebook inbox. That's a major problem. Why? Without the e-mail, if your members don't regularly check their Facebook inbox they might not even realize they received a group-related message.

This is a major drawback of Facebook groups. When your group has fewer than 5,000 members, you have an extremely effective way of communicating with them. But once you cross the 5,000-member threshold, you lose that functionality and never get it back—unless you remove members to stay under that 5,000 limit (which some people do, by the way). It gets

217

even worse with pages. As a page admin, there is no way to send a "message" to your fans. You can only send "updates." So what's an update? In your Facebook inbox, there are "messages" and "updates." The default tab is messages and very few people read the updates. That means an update sent to your fans will get read by almost nobody.

If you want to communicate with your Facebook page fans, the best way to do it is to post on your page's wall. Wall posts go into the Facebook user's news feed and end up getting seen way more than updates. So let's take a minute and talk about wall posts. Whether you're posting on your profile wall, your group wall, or your page wall, the primary objective is interaction. Interaction leads to trust, and trust is an essential precursor to the purchase decision. You need trust first, and the fastest way to get it is by encouraging interaction.

One of the simplest things you can do when posting on your wall is to end your post with a question. What do you think? Any suggestions? Are we missing anything? Other ideas? How can we help? Who's your favorite? What went wrong? Ah, yes. The power of a question! Questions tug at people's subconscious. They beg for a response. They tickle people's minds and invite new ideas. Bottom line: they encourage interaction. Using this one simple strategy will dramatically increase the effectiveness of your Facebook activity. And on your Facebook page, interaction is absolutely essential for building a broader fan base. Keep in mind that any time Facebook users make a comment on your page wall, that activity is also noted on *their* wall. That means their network is notified. It means their interaction spurs a viral process that can attract new fans. The more interaction you have, the more people find out about your page.

If you're just getting started, your first milestone should be getting 300 fans. Once you have 300 or more fans, you'll notice that your number of fans will start to grow on its own, especially if you're actively encouraging interaction on your posts. Also, when people comment on your post, they're automatically subscribed to subsequent comments. That means they're notified when other people comment after them. So you can post something, accumulate a bunch of comments from interested fans, and then comment again yourself, knowing everyone will see your follow-up comment. These strategies are simple. It just boils down to a series of simple little tricks to maximize your effectiveness. It's all about understanding platforms like Facebook and how they work and then leveraging them to achieve your objectives. Once you're comfortable with the process, it's easy.

Implementation Checklist

☐ Log into Facebook and visit your inbox.
☐ Notice the "messages" and "updates" tabs.
☐ If you have a page, send an "update."
☐ Measure the response you get.
☐ Next, post something on the page wall.
☐ Measure the response you get.
☐ Always end wall posts with a question.
☐ Add follow-up comments on wall posts.
☐ Compare notes and ideas with a colleague.

Chapter 73

Facebook
Biggest Opportunity

What's the biggest opportunity on Facebook?

Tagging people on photos. Tagging people on photos has such huge potential and is so underutilized. Here's how it works. Let's say I take a photo of Susie, upload it to my Facebook page, and then tag her in the photo. What happens? Well, the photo shows up on my Facebook page. That's where I uploaded it to. But it also shows up in Susie's profile as "photos uploaded by others." That means I can put a photo into Susie's profile. Think about that! The photo also goes onto Susie's wall. It says "Susie was tagged in a photo" and the photo will be there for her entire network to see.

Last year, I worked with a small winery. It was a very small family-owned operation and we hosted a public wine tasting to try and get more exposure for the place. We only charged a $5 entrance fee and marketed the event using offline channels. Lots of people showed up. When they entered, we had a table set up where they had to register. At that same table, they received their wineglass (included) and also got their first pour. So when they left the registration table, they already had wine in a wine-glass. A few feet away, we had an area where the winery name and logo was displayed on the wall, and a photographer greeted people there. "Welcome. We're thrilled you're here. We'd love to take your photo. Is that okay?" Almost everyone said yes.

Think about these photos. They all had people smiling with wine in their hands and the name and logo of the winery in the background. These were *branded* photographs. That's very important. They were basically

220

advertisements! Right? I mean, it's subtle but those photos were ads. After the event, we uploaded all the photos to the winery's newly introduced Facebook page and tagged everybody. You need to be friends with people before you can tag them in photos so we gave everyone a full explanation of the process at the tasting. We had to send friend requests first but that was a small price to pay for the end result! We had about 180 photos and ended up with more than 100 people tagged. So those photos ended up in the profiles of more than 100 people. We basically put an advertisement into all of their profiles! Not only that, but the photos also appeared on the walls of those same 100 people. The awareness shot up immediately and the foot traffic increased the very next weekend.

Where do you interact with your customers or prospects? At trade shows? At a retail storefront? At events you host? Think about the opportunities you might have to take photos and tag people on Facebook. If you're a real estate agent and you sell a house, you need to take a picture of your customers in front of the house and that "SOLD" sign. If you're a contractor and just did a major renovation of someone's kitchen, you need to take a picture of your happy customers in front of those beautiful granite countertops!

I worked with a shop that does pedicures for women. They started taking photos of these women's feet and tagging them. You couldn't even see the women's faces. You only saw their feet with little flowers painted on their toenails. Before they uploaded the photos to Facebook, they brought them into Photoshop and added in their company name and phone number, subtly in the top right-hand corner. Over time, they accumulated dozens of photos—or advertisements—in the profiles of their customers.

Think about this stuff. How can you leverage it?

As a speaker, I create images of the cities I speak in with my head shot superimposed at the top. I add text explaining which conference I'm speaking at and the date. I upload the images to my page and tag myself in each one, bringing them into my profile as well. Whether you want to admit it or not, people are looking at your photos on Facebook. That's what people do. People love photos. So when they're looking at my photos, they see these images of cities all around the world. Without ever speaking to me, they see where I have spoken. It builds my credibility.

Tag people in branded photos. Find ways to capture your customers and prospects in situations that involve your products or services. If you do it once or twice, it won't change your business one bit. But if you accumulate dozens or even hundreds of these photos, it'll change your business forever.

Implementation Checklist

- ☐ Where do you interact with customers?
- ☐ Where could you interact with prospects?
- ☐ Take photos that involve your products.
- ☐ Bring the photos into Photoshop.
- ☐ Subtly add your contact information.
- ☐ Upload the photos to your Facebook page.
- ☐ Tag the people featured in each photo.
- ☐ Do this regularly, accumulating photos.
- ☐ Compare notes and ideas with a colleague.

Chapter 74

Facebook
Places and Deals

Is your business on Facebook Places?

The hottest trend on today's social Internet is local check-in. It all started with Foursquare, a mobile application allowing users to "check-in" at local businesses. Anyway, it was so successful that Yelp jumped on board with the same functionality. Google was next to express interest (although not yet released) and now Facebook has joined the party as well. What makes this so significant? Facebook is the most popular social network on the Internet and already has an active established user base. So their introduction of Facebook Places—offering the same check-in functionality to Facebook users—sent shockwaves. Better yet, the platform is built on Facebook pages, providing all local businesses a powerful incentive to create pages for themselves.

In order to fully take advantage of Facebook Places, you'll have to claim your Place and verify that you're the business owner. If you're unsure if your business is already on Facebook (it may have been added by someone else), search for your business name in the standard search bar. If you're already there, visit the page and click "Is this your business?" If you're not included yet, click "check-in" and then "add" on the left-hand side.

Facebook Places is pretty cool but they went a step further. They introduced Facebook "Deals" so businesses can offer discounts, promotions, and bonuses to people who check-in at their establishments. I'm not suggesting similar promotions aren't available elsewhere (like Foursquare and Yelp among others) but the enormous user base on Facebook magnifies the opportunity.

It's important to note that Facebook Places (allowing check-in) and Deals are primarily available on mobile phones. However, you can also access a stripped-down version on a regular computer by visiting:

http://touch.facebook.com

There are four different types of "Deals" that businesses can offer on Facebook.

1. *Individual Deals.* Businesses can offer one-time deals. Customers who check-in at the business location could receive something special.
2. *Friends Deals.* Businesses can offer incentives and discounts to groups of people (up to eight people) who check-in together.
3. *Loyalty Deals.* Businesses can offer incentives after a given customer has checked in multiple times (ranging from 2 to 20 check-ins).
4. *Charity Deals.* Businesses can offer a donation to a preselected charity every time someone checks in.

Whether you're using these mobile applications or not, I guarantee some of your customers are. Create an Individual Deal for your users. I recommend offering something significant at the beginning. It'll show you how many of your customers are using this functionality. Once you get a feel for the audience it reaches, you can calibrate your deal more carefully. Here are a few tips for creating effective deals. First, make sure all your employees are aware of what you're offering. Second, make your deal as simple as possible. There is no such thing as a confused buyer. Ensure it's clear and simple. Third, make the deal easy to redeem.

By the way, get your smart phone out, open the Facebook application, and click "Places" and then "Check-in" to see places near your current location. The ones with Individual, Friends, or Loyalty Deals will be identified with a square yellow icon. The ones with Charity Deals will be identified with a green icon. Click on a few (even if you don't need their products or services) and see what these businesses are doing.

Change your deals from time to time. Don't let them get stale. Why not have a different deal every week or every month? Test it. See what works. Give your deals a deadline. Limited-time offers always get more attention than perpetual promotions. Even if you don't have a local business, check-in and see what deals are being offered nearby. You'll probably save some money or receive some cool stuff. It's amazing how many deals are already available. It's almost like a parallel world—a hidden network you never knew about . . . until now.

Facebook Places and Deals will explode in the coming years. Mark my words. It's just too easy. And businesses unaware of the functionality will be at an increasing disadvantage over time. Claim your business on Facebook Places and create a Deal today.

Implementation Checklist

- ☐ Open the Facebook app on your phone.
- ☐ Click on "Places" and then "Check-in."
- ☐ Notice the businesses listed nearby.
- ☐ See which have green or yellow icons.
- ☐ Make sure your business is listed.
- ☐ Verify that you're the business owner.
- ☐ Offer a "deal" to people who check-in.
- ☐ Individual Deals: one-time offers.
- ☐ Friends Deals: groups of people (up to 8).
- ☐ Loyalty Deals: multiple check-ins.
- ☐ Charity Deals: donations for check-ins.
- ☐ Compare notes and ideas with a colleague.

Chapter 75

YouTube
Viral Content

What's the most effective type of content?

Before we answer that, we have to determine what the options are. There are basically just four types of content available: text, audio, photos (or images), and video (or animation). Which do you think is the most effective from a marketing perspective? You guessed it. Video! People love video. Period. It's easy. It's intuitive. It's fun. Video requires the least amount of effort to watch, understand, and/or learn from. As a result, good video content tends to get shared more than other types of content.

Next up: where does your marketing content come from? Well, there are really just two places where relevant marketing content can come from: your business or your customers. Think about this for a minute. Peer reviews: that's content about your company provided by your customers. What about photos? Yes, you could be sharing photos of your business online, but your customers might be posting photos about your business too. What about videos? Same thing.

What's more effective, content provided by your business or content provided by your customers? Right again! Content provided by your customers is far more effective than content provided by your own business. It makes sense. People will always believe what someone else says about you more than what you say about yourself. It's more credible. It's a third-party endorsement, whether it's a positive comment or a negative one. So what's the most effective content available? Bingo! Video content about your business that is provided by your customers is the most effective content you can get.

Back in January 2009, the Australian Tourism Board advertised for "The Best Job in the World." It got huge media coverage. Maybe you remember it. The job paid $100,000 for six months—not bad. The successful candidate would live in a beautiful house on an island in Australia's Great Barrier Reef area. He or she would be provided with all the snorkeling gear, scuba diving apparatus, and parasailing equipment he or she could handle. The responsibilities? Simple. He or she would have to write one blog post every day on the Australian Tourism Board's blog.

In order to apply, candidates had to submit a video (one minute or less) demonstrating why they would be perfect for the job. Well, as you can imagine, the buzz exploded and the job opportunity was reported by media outlets around the world. The result? Almost 35,000 people submitted videos. Talk about spectacular content! We're talking about almost 35,000 videos featuring beautiful young human beings (for the most part) talking about why they love the Great Barrier Reef. Brilliant. All those videos were posted on YouTube and collectively watched by millions of people around the world. Awesome, awesome, awesome!

But it gets better. People were allowed to vote on the videos they liked best—one vote per e-mail address. So they ended up with an opt-in list of more than 400,000 e-mail addresses. The brilliance of this campaign is insane. The interesting thing is that the eventual 6-month contract wasn't nearly as successful as the campaign to hire the candidate in the first place. The hiring campaign delivered most of the benefit. That kind of video exposure is priceless.

I recently met with a company that makes accessories for wheelchairs. They make a great product that make it possible for wheelchair users to move forward by either pushing or pulling vertical levers instead of manually turning the wheels. We put together a brilliant strategy based on the same concept as the Australian Tourism Board. Unfortunately, the company never pulled the trigger, but I'm convinced it would've been a winner. The idea was to send e-mails to their past customers letting them know we'd be having a contest where owners of these accessories could submit videos of how they were using the product. The most creative and inspiring videos would win great prizes. The plan was to purchase 20 Flip digital video recorders and send them out to interested customers along with self-addressed postage-paid return envelopes. "Record your video and send it back," the insert would say. I bet we would've gotten some fabulous videos.

I could imagine a video of someone (maybe a veteran) using the levers to propel himself up Lombard Street in San Francisco, the steepest street in the country. Or someone going up a hiking trail . . . in a wheelchair! It's really too bad we never got a chance to test the strategy. How can you incentivize your own customers to create content about your business? Give them a good reason (like contest prizes) and you'll be amazed at what you get back.

Implementation Checklist

- ☐ What do you do that's remarkable?
- ☐ How can your customers tell their story?
- ☐ Imagine videos about your business.
- ☐ Incentivize your customers to make them.
- ☐ Have a contest and offer great prizes.
- ☐ Support the process by providing cameras.
- ☐ Post and promote those videos on YouTube.
- ☐ Compare notes and ideas with a colleague.

Chapter 76

YouTube
Demonstrate Expertise

Are you building exposure on YouTube?

YouTube is serving more than two billion video views per day right now. Are any of those videos yours? Are any of those videos about your business? Those two billion views are being watched whether you're there or not. People with questions are searching on YouTube whether you're providing answers or not. So how do we get your content in front of that traffic? How do we get your business in front of those eyeballs?

You may be familiar with the name Gary Vaynerchuk. If not, we're talking about a super high-energy and fast-talking 31-year-old guy who inherited his parents' retail wine store in New Jersey, just outside New York City. The store is called WineLibrary. So what did he do? He started his own video blog called WineLibrary TV and his frantic communication style make his videos extremely entertaining to watch. He literally eats dirt and chews leather to explain the flavors in wine. He's not exactly your typical French sommelier! But the younger generation loves this guy.

To be clear, Gary Vaynerchuk posts a new video almost every single day, so this is no small undertaking. But he managed to explode his annual revenue from $4 million to more than $60 million in the process. Imagine: $4 million to more than $60 million!! And two thirds of the revenue came from online orders. His parents never once took an online order. He introduced that. Two thirds of $60 million is $40 million! This guy went from zero to $40 million in online orders! How? He demonstrated his expertise in a clever way in the middle of a raging river. You've heard this before. These stories are always the same.

Consider Blentec, a company that manufactures commercial and residential blenders. As the story goes, the newly hired marketing manager, George Wright, was walking through the factory one day and noticed the CEO, Tom Dickson, trying to destroy a 2×2 block of wood with an entry-level residential blender. He succeeded. The room was littered with sawdust and chips of wood. Apparently, he did that on a regular basis. It was his way of testing the durability of their products.

George saw the potential immediately. They needed to record it on video! So they started a series called "Will it blend?" to share the results on YouTube. The start-up costs for the campaign totaled just $85. They started blending all sorts of things. They blended marbles. They blended golf balls. They blended a full size rake! And they also blended an iPhone. Yes, it's true. They blended an iPhone and it got completely destroyed. It literally turned to dust. On the video, they called it "iDust."

What were the results? Sales didn't double. Sales didn't triple. Sales soared 500 percent! Why? They demonstrated the capabilities of their product in a clever way in the middle of a raging river. It's always the same. Bottom line: It worked because it was remarkable! What do you do that's remarkable? What do you do in your business that's remarkable?

A woman recently attended a conference where I spoke and she e-mailed me a few days later, all excited. Her business sells premium foods like caviar, truffle mushrooms, and foie gras and she wanted to create a video about her business and put it on YouTube. "A video." One video. Why stop at just one video when her company sold 85 products? I told her she should make 85 videos—one for each product! And then optimize each video for the relevant keywords for that particular product.

She never made all 85 videos but she did make 27 of them, and they were all optimized for highly specific keyword phrases like "black truffle oil." People are searching for that stuff. They found her videos and each one pointed back to her website. She racked up more than 25,000 views in her first 12 months and her revenue doubled.

When I launched the first edition of this book, I recorded 57 videos, one for almost every chapter (the original book had only 60 chapters). I set up the camera in my office and recorded one chapter after another, and then chopped up the footage into separate videos later. A good friend of mine told me I should change my clothes in between each video. No! Nobody is going to watch all 57 videos. They're only going to watch *one*. Each video is optimized for different keywords, based on what that particular chapter is about. So people searching for information on YouTube will find one of my videos and each one points back to my website. Mission accomplished.

What do you do that's remarkable? What's the area where your customers are most fascinated? Where do they give you the most animated response? That's it! Get that on video. Share that on YouTube. Pick an angle or a gimmick to make your videos unique. There are basically three different strategies for creating videos: educate, entertain, or shock.

1. *Educate.* The fastest growing content on YouTube is educational how-to content. Every day, the demand for valuable how-to content increases. Teach your prospects how to use your products or services. Teach them how to avoid common mistakes. Teach them about the tips, tricks, and tools that will make their lives easier.

2. *Entertain.* People love to be entertained. Humor will always get a warm welcome from YouTube users. Show your prospects the humor in your industry. Show them the irony in your products or services. Find ways to make people laugh while engaging them about your value proposition. Gary Vaynerchuk basically chose a combination of education and entertainment and enjoyed enormous success in the process.

3. *Shock.* You want viral? Shock people. We've all seen examples of this approach. The "Will it blend?" campaign by Blentec essentially falls into this category. Their demonstrations were shocking, albeit with some great entertainment sprinkled in. What's shocking about your product or service? How can you shock your prospects with the results you deliver?

Regardless of which direction you choose, YouTube offers a tremendous opportunity to those who share video content. Find a way to participate with your own business.

Implementation Checklist

- ☐ Demonstrate your expertise on YouTube.
- ☐ Display the capabilities of your product.
- ☐ Exhibit the benefits of your service.
- ☐ Identify what you do that's remarkable.
- ☐ Upload new videos regularly.
- ☐ Educate: provide how-to information.
- ☐ Entertain: show the humor in your field.
- ☐ Shock: surprise viewers with wild videos.
- ☐ Compare notes and ideas with a colleague.

Chapter 77

YouTube
Video Promotion

Are your YouTube videos getting 100,000 views?

Everybody wants their videos to "go viral." They want the video to catch on and spread like wildfire, accumulating hundreds of thousands of views along the way. Turns out, getting a video to "go viral" is hard work. Don't get me wrong. There are definitely some videos that just hit it right. They strike a chord and get shared around the globe. But there are also countless great videos that get a few hundred views and then fade out. To give a video the best possible odds of becoming successful, you need to give it a good push at the beginning. There are lots of things you can do to promote YouTube videos and there are companies that specialize in doing just that. What are they doing?

First, make sure the video isn't too long. These days, we live in an ADHD society. Nobody has any patience anymore. Most of the successful "viral" videos are between 30 and 45 seconds long. As a rule of thumb, your videos should be no longer than three or four minutes.

Second, ping your network. Once your video is uploaded with an effective title, description, and tags, send it out to your e-mail list. Post it on Facebook. Tweet about it. People enjoy videos and will often take a few minutes to watch yours, if invited. That will get you some initial views.

Third, encourage comments—right on the video itself! Near the end of your video, ask people to leave comments below. Ask them a question. Ask for their input. Also, invite controversy. Controversy leads to more comments and comments improve YouTube rankings.

Fourth, find a high-traffic forum that's related to your video's topic and embed your video in a new thread. Use an enticing title and encourage posts. The longer your thread (and video) are in the "fast water" (see Chapter 53 for full instructions) the more views it'll rack up. In many cases, you can get a few hundred or a few thousand views by effectively managing your thread on the forum.

Fifth, do the same thing on two or three other forums. These are all independent communities and you can double or triple your results by repeating the exact same steps on multiple communities. Post your video on Facebook Groups and LinkedIn Groups and Google Groups and Yahoo! Groups. Post it anywhere your target audience spends time.

The companies that specialize in this sort of thing generally maintain multiple accounts on all these various platforms, including YouTube itself. By doing so, they can start the initial dialog (via comments) and controversy all by themselves. They can also keep their forum threads active and popular within those communities. Understandably, YouTube tries to limit these types of artificial conversations and will automatically check to see if the various accounts are being managed from the same IP address. That means you'd have to have people in different locations using different Internet connections to do this safely.

My advice? Be careful. It's important you understand what people are doing. That's your competition. Whether you decide to employ similar techniques yourself (or hire a company that uses these strategies) is entirely up to you. My objective is to give you a clear picture of how these things happen and then leave the final decision up to you. Ideally, you want your video to make it onto the "Most Popular" pages on YouTube. They're featured on the homepage and show the trending videos each day. There are a variety of factors that determine which videos make the cut, including the numbers of views and comments. The point is that once you get to the "Most Popular" pages, your views soar.

At the end of the day, you work like crazy to get the first few thousand views, and then you get the next 50,000 for free. Once you're on the "Most Popular" pages, the exposure explodes. And *that's* when you'll find out if the video has true viral potential. Once you get to that point, the video is circulated widely enough to really take off . . . or not. Some will go to 100,000 views. Others will go to 1,500,000 views. It all depends on the video. Is it catchy? Is it educational? Is it funny? Is it shocking? If so, you could be in for an exciting ride. By the way, once your video gets a bunch of views, YouTube will offer to "monetize" it with advertisements, giving you a share of the revenue. If your channel does well in general, they'll offer you an opportunity to become a "YouTube Partner." Both will result in revenue and exposure.

Moral: promote your videos! It can change your business.

Implementation Checklist

- ☐ Make your videos short.
- ☐ After uploading, tell all your friends.
- ☐ Post it on Facebook and e-mail your list.
- ☐ Ask for comments—right on the video!
- ☐ Create a thread on a high-traffic forum.
- ☐ Embed your video and invite interaction.
- ☐ Post it to Facebook and LinkedIn groups
- ☐ Post it to Yahoo! and Google groups.
- ☐ Try to get it on the "Most Popular" pages.
- ☐ If you succeed, sit back and enjoy the ride.
- ☐ Compare notes and ideas with a colleague.

Chapter 78

Social Media Monitoring

Who's talking about your business?

Maybe nobody. This book is designed to change that. Most of the strategies we've covered in this book are designed to get that conversation started. But for larger businesses and even a lot of smaller ones, there may already be people sharing their opinions in the public domain. That's where social media monitoring comes in. Social media monitoring basically refers to listening. It refers to the job of staying on top of that ongoing conversation with the intention of contributing your own comments and insights to the dialog, appreciating positive comments and addressing negative ones. There are a number of tools that can help you monitor that online conversation and we'll be reviewing a few of them in this chapter.

Google Alerts

It's the most basic but still one of the best. Every single small business and self-employed service professional should be using Google Alerts to stay on top of relevant listings as they appear online. (Refer to Chapter 11 for more detailed instructions for leveraging this valuable tool.)

Twitter Advanced Search

You can get very detailed search results by effectively using the Twitter Search feature. By clicking the "advanced search" link, you'll have access to a variety of options that can help you refine your query. It's a great way to see what people are saying about you and/or your company. (Refer back to Chapter 65 for more information about Twitter Search.)

Addictomatic

This tool aggregates search results from Digg, Flickr, blogs, Twitter, Google BlogSearch, Bing, and more, and presents it all on a single page. It also provides you with a URL to that page, dynamically updating search results every time you visit. Check it out and enter your name in quotation marks and you'll quickly get a snapshot of where you're showing up.

Social Mention

This monitoring tool goes a step further and provides metrics on passion, sentiment, reach, and strength. If you're just getting started, this can be a bit sobering. It certainly was for me. But it'll also leave you with new ideas for where to invest your time as well as information on the impact your current efforts are having.

HootSuite

HootSuite has evolved into a powerful dashboard, not only for managing multiple Twitter profiles but also for distributing content to a variety of other platforms. Does that qualify as a monitoring tool? Maybe not. But its increasing functionality and broad user base make it impossible to ignore.

Seesmic

Seesmic has a lot of the same functionality as HootSuite and you certainly don't need to be using both of them. But for fear of incorrectly recommending one over the other, I am including both. Try each one and pick the one you like better. It's worth mentioning, however, that Seesmic recently purchased Ping.fm, dramatically expanding their distribution capabilities.

ScoutLabs

Here's where we start spending money. ScoutLabs isn't free but it provides impressive functionality including workflow and response management. If you have a team of people monitoring your social media presence, this tool will help manage that process. The interface also delivers valuable insights on sentiment tracking and volume trending. Also, it allows users to "private label" the interface and provide restricted access to clients, making it ideal for consultants, freelancers, and agencies.

Radian6

This is the powerhouse. Radian6 is designed for larger businesses and has extensive workflow management features and a sophisticated dashboard. Not only will the insights and metrics make you look like a rock star, but they can be disseminated through integrated workflows and customizable alerts. For corporations needing to manage an active social media presence, Radian6 is a great option.

Regardless of what you decide to use, remember that listening is a lot more important than talking on today's social Internet. People are often impressed when a representative from the company responds to a comment they made online. It also introduces you to prospects you may not have known about otherwise.

Implementation Checklist

- ☐ Make sure you listen first and talk second.
- ☐ Experiment with Google Alerts.
- ☐ Experiment with Twitter Advanced Search.
- ☐ Experiment with Addictomatic.
- ☐ Experiment with Social Mention.
- ☐ Experiment with Hootsuite.
- ☐ Experiment with Seesmic.
- ☐ Read and learn about ScoutLabs ($$).
- ☐ Read and learn about Radian6 ($$$).
- ☐ Compare notes and ideas with a colleague.

Part Seven

Conclusions and Execution

Chapter 79

Wow Your Audience

So . . . how's your business doing?

We're approaching the finish line and we've covered a lot of different topics. Now, it's time to pull it all together. It's time to wow your Internet audience. It's time to show them how solid your online identity has become. This book has introduced a lot of strategies to build exposure and gain credibility online. Hopefully, you've tried a few. If so, you already have a number of profiles on various online platforms along with little demonstrations of your expertise on each. Cross-reference everything!

If you published a few articles on EzineArticles, link to your "expert author" page. If you've been posting comments on popular online forums, link to your profile. If you uploaded some videos to YouTube, link to your channel. And if your press releases were picked up by major media websites, link to those stories. Also, put links to your Twitter feed, your Friend-Feed account, and your Facebook and LinkedIn profiles. Post links to your profiles on social bookmarking platforms like Digg, Delicious, and StumbleUpon. When people land on your website, you want them to be blown away with all the things you're doing online. You want e-mails that say "you're everywhere!" We've covered a lot in this book. Now, it's time to wow your audience with all that progress.

Of course, the final objective is to make money. That's what we're all trying to do. At the beginning of the book, we spent some time defining your business model, organizing your content, and packaging your value. There was a chapter about writing effective sales copy for your products or services. Now, the job shifts to one of calibration. Monitor your traffic and see where your website visitors are coming from. Check your Google Analytics regularly and see where people are coming from and where they're spending time on your website. Calibrate your activities to optimize results.

Here are the most common weak links that diminish the effectiveness of your online presence:

- ◆ Low or inconsistent website traffic
- ◆ Low sign-up rates for intermediate content
- ◆ Low open rates on e-mails (subject lines)
- ◆ Low conversion on e-mails (sales copy)
- ◆ Website doesn't engage visitors or build trust
- ◆ Low conversion on website sales copy
- ◆ Products don't provide sufficient value

Measure each of these areas and commit to a process of continuous improvement. You can double your business by doubling the effectiveness of just *one* of these areas. If you double the effectiveness of *two,* your business could increase fourfold. If you double the effectiveness of *three,* your business could jump eightfold. Running a business in the Internet age isn't rocket science. It's a process. And once you learn it, you can do it again and again. It all begins with demonstrating your expertise, providing value, and building trust. After that, you invite your audience to review your advanced content and (hopefully) buy something.

I sincerely hope you can use this book as a guide to grow your business on the Internet. Please keep me posted on your progress. Send me an e-mail. I love hearing success stories!

Implementation Checklist

- ☐ Make a list of all your online profiles.
- ☐ Wherever possible, link them all together.
- ☐ Show your audience what you have done.
- ☐ Always look for opportunities to integrate.
- ☐ Keep track of your successes and failures.
- ☐ Please keep me posted on your progress.
- ☐ Compare notes and ideas with a colleague.

Chapter 80

Consistency Wins

One of the most common reactions I get from readers is that they feel over-whelmed and don't know how to incorporate all these strategies into their daily schedule. As with any process, there are two aspects to a successful implementation. The first involves all the set-up work and the second involves the ongoing maintenance work that keeps the strategies engaged. The set-up work is awful. It's frustrating. It's infuriating. "Where's my photo?" "This link doesn't work!" "Where's the text I just uploaded?" We've all been there. But once the set-up work is complete, the maintenance work is much easier.

When starting a new project, *expect* chaos at first. Expect disaster. Expect frustration. But also take comfort knowing that three hours later, when you've finally figured it out, you'll have one more layer of online activity—one more layer of credibility—in place. Initiate one new project each week. Maybe you can do it on Friday afternoon when you're not as busy as the rest of the week. One by one, you can endure the frustration and tackle another strategy, each one adding another layer to the mix.

Marketing reminds me of expensive sports cars. These sports cars often have ten or more layers of paint—maybe five layers of color and another five of clear gloss. Together, all those layers create an incredible finish. Marketing is similar. You have to pile layer on top of layer on top of layer. Put your content in every raging river you can find. Keep piling more stuff on. Build a truly massive online identity. And eventually, it takes on a life of its own. People find you in one place and then see that you're active every-where else as well. Often, they're blown away. How did they *not* know about you before? You're everywhere! Your overwhelming online presence

243

establishes immediate credibility and your prospects become customers much more quickly.

Like everything in life, discipline and consistency define success. Don't try to do too much at the beginning. You'll burn yourself out. Instead, pick a slow and steady pace, a pace you're comfortable with. The runners leading a marathon at the 10-mile mark rarely win in the end. Don't get frustrated if your phone doesn't ring during the first week. Building trust and credibility takes time. But if you keep at it, you'll accumulate more and more content and the situation will soon change.

At the beginning, someone might notice you and find three blog posts, two articles, and a video on YouTube. That's not enough to overwhelm anyone. It's a good start but it's not going to close the sale. A year later, someone else notices you and finds 30 blog posts, 25 articles, and 15 educational videos, not to mention dozens of "expert author" citations on Google and maybe even a podcast on iTunes. Now, *that's* a different story. The trust comes a lot quicker.

What about another year down the road? Now, your blog is massive and you have followers on all the major social media platforms. Your content is featured in hundreds of different places and you have become a recognized authority in your field. Now the roles are reversed. You can pick who you want to work with. That *is* possible. Build your online identity consistently over time and you'll be amazed at what starts to happen. Stick with it. Trust that your efforts will deliver results in the long run. The eventual payoff is well worth the effort. I promise.

Thank you for reading this book. If you found it useful, please tell your friends and business colleagues about it. Your endorsement is worth far more than my own marketing efforts.

About the Author

Patrick Schwerdtfeger experienced the power of the Internet firsthand. In 2006, he recorded 17 podcasts about the mortgage business. With very little promotion, those podcasts accumulated over 75,000 downloads in 27 countries. Why? Because they provided value and were positioned in the middle of high-traffic websites like iTunes.

He has followed the same winning formula multiple times, accumulating over 25,000 followers on Twitter and 100,000 views on YouTube. This simple process of providing value on high-traffic websites has resulted in a steady increase in his credibility, audience, and income, and the same strategy can be used by anyone.

Today, Patrick is a regular speaker for Bloomberg TV and is the author of *Webify Your Business: Internet Marketing Secrets for the Self-Employed* (2009) and *Make Yourself Useful: Marketing in the 21st Century* (2008). He has spoken about Modern Entrepreneurship and the Social Media Revolution at conferences and conventions around the world.

Index